Branch Living:

Your Guide to Putting Faith in Life and Life in Faith

LISA SCHNEDLER

Scriptures marked NIV are taken from the NEW INTERNATIONAL VERSION (NIV):Scripture taken from THE HOLY BIBLE, NEW INTERNATIONAL VERSION ®. Copyright©1973, 1978, 1984, 2011 by Biblica, Inc.™. Used by permission of Zondervan

ISBN: 978-1-945975-38-7

Published by EA Books Publishing a division of Living Parables of Central Florida, Inc. a 501c3 EABooksPublishing.com

CONTENTS

A Note from the Author

This book is for you, if:

You know there is more you could be doing with your life.
You are tired of living a life that feels like someone else's.
You feel you aren't using your gifts.
You are afraid you will "die with your music in you."

I also have felt like this.

But, I have learned the way out.
It is Branch Living.

What is Branch Living?

It isn't a formula.
It's not a method.

It's a pathway.

If you follow the steps in this book, you will find joy. Your life will have more meaning. You will use your gifts more fully. You will have richer relationships. You will know you are living a life that matters.

Your life will not be perfect — no one's life is — but you will have joy and a sense of direction.

You might be asking how I can make such a claim. I do so with great confidence because I didn't develop this path — I discovered it. And now that I have, I want to share it with you.

I discovered this path by reaching a point in my life when I felt overwhelmed, unfulfilled, and exhausted. I was a Christian, but I was still trying to live my life on my own terms, believing if I just worked harder, longer, tried more, everything would work out. I wore a heavy yoke and came to a point where I just simply could no longer bear it.

As I said, I didn't create this path, nor am I the first one to walk it. God, who created you and me, laid out a perfect pathway for us. He will walk along with us, but we need to take the steps.

The acronym "BRANCH" helps keep these steps in focus. It also defines our status as Christ followers.

Jesus tells us:

"I am the vine; you are the branches. If you remain in me and I in you, you will bear much fruit; apart from me you can do nothing. If you do not remain in me, you are like a branch that is thrown away and withers; such branches are picked up, thrown into the fire and burned. If you remain in me and my words remain in you, ask whatever you wish, and it will be done for you. This is to my Father's glory, that you bear much fruit, showing yourselves to be my disciples" (John 15: 5-8)

God keeps His promises, and by following this path, you will bear fruit!

Branch Living has six components:

B — Bonding with God
R — Relationships
A — Almsgiving
N — New/ Renewed dreams and Desires and Community – The Calling
C — Church
H — Habits

We will explore each of these steps in the chapters to come. Although you can work through the steps on your own, it is best to work with friends or a small group such as a Bible study or church group. Branch Living, by its very design, is meant to be done in community.

Let's begin!

Introduction: Why Branch Living?

You may be like me. You may have tried many trendy ways to revamp your life, to lose weight, or to be a better parent or spouse. You may have geared yourself up for real change this time – then failed, your confidence sinking a bit lower.

Branch Living is different. I promise. It is a series of steps on how to apply the greatest book ever written to your life. And, like its Author, it allows for failure and restarts. It doesn't matter where you are right now. Branch Living will make your life better.

The fact that you have picked up this book and that you have read this far means that you are ready to make a change. Branch Living will give you the tools to succeed!

Here is how it works:

You work on your personal goals in each of six areas:
- **Bonding** (with God)
- **Relationships** (developing new ones or strengthening the ones you have)
- **Almsgiving** (giving of your time, gifts, and talents)
- **New** (or renewed) dreams for you and/or your community
- **Church**
- **Habits**

You set your goals following reflection and prayer, and then you work toward them. When you fail, there is an easy way to get back on track. When you succeed, you get a reward! And though the goals and plans are yours and yours alone, Branch Living will give you the support you need. You get in-person support through the network of groups we are developing and through our online community, planned conferences, email support, and many other avenues.

I quote many gifted individuals throughout this book who offer pithy insights. But, most importantly, I quote the true Author of the wisdom behind this book:

"I lift my eyes to the mountains -- where does my help come? My help comes from the Lord, the Maker of heaven and earth." (Psalm 121:1-2)

"For I know the plans I have for you," declares the Lord, "plans to prosper you and not to harm you, plans to give you hope and a future." (Jeremiah 29:11)

When I am reading a book on life planning or self-improvement, I like to start with an overview — a snapshot — of what I am about to read so I can learn for whom the book is written and what its purpose is. I will start by providing this information.

Whom: This book is geared toward Christians and toward those who would like to become followers of Christ. The power behind Branch Living is our bond with Christ. But Branch Living is for everyone who wishes to use it. It is my prayer that if you use these tools, you will discover the Power behind the tools.

What: The aim of this book is to help you move toward your life's purpose, which is God-given. It assists you by providing an easy-to-use system for keeping your goals in the forefront, tracking your success, supporting your efforts, and encouraging you along the way.

When: The best time to start Branch Living is whenever you are motivated to make changes in your life.

How: Branch Living begins by teaching the importance of our bond with God. In order to thrive, we need the nourishment, "living water," grounding, and foundation only He can provide. Once well grafted into this Vine (God), you will explore the unique purpose He has placed in your life to further His Kingdom on earth.

Each of us works out our purpose in life by the choices we make with our time every day, week, month, and year. We choose how we nurture our relationships, how we spend our money and time, what we do to renew our lives and the community around us, and how we engage with our churches. Our daily habits move us forward or backward in our growth and development. In Branch Living, we focus on each of these areas:

- **B**onding—Bonding with God through His Son, Jesus Christ
- **R**elationships—Maintaining healthy relationships with our family, friends, fellow believers, coworkers, and everyone who is within our "orb"
- **A**lmsgiving—Giving of our money and time
- **N**ew (Renew)—Working to make ourselves and our world new, redeemed, and vibrant
- **C**hurch—Engaging with our local churches
- **H**abits—Making choices that move us forward

These are the building blocks of Branch Living.

Come with us!

Chapter 1

Bonding with God

"I am the vine, you are the branches. If you remain in me and I in you, you will bear much fruit; apart from me you can do nothing."
John 15:5

Did you know that God loves you exactly as you are? He knows your heart; He knows your life story—the good and the bad and all you have done and failed to do. And, still He loves you. Just as you are.

God is gracious—He does not force Himself on us, but waits to be invited into our lives.

As He tells us in Scripture:

"Here I am! I stand at the door and knock. If anyone hears my voice and opens the door, I will come in and eat with that person, and they with me."
Revelations 3:20

God wants to be in relationship with us. He always takes the first step toward us, but to have a relationship, we must also take a step toward Him. Have you taken this step?

Perhaps you have heard God knocking on the door of your heart. Listen. Take time to listen to the voice of God calling you. Most people don't know that they are spiritually asleep until they awaken to the spiritual life. You will never know what is possible — what you were designed to do and achieve — until you answer that call from God. God is the master potter, and we are the clay. If we place ourselves in His care and ask Him to direct our lives, He will turn our lives into masterpieces. Without Him, we remain lumps of clay.

Maybe you are already a Christ follower, and you are seeking to serve Him in a deeper way. Or, perhaps you have turned away from God and want to come back to Him. God is calling you to Himself today — no matter what you have done in your life. God calls each of us. The choice to respond is ours. Our relationship with God is a love affair, a relationship that deepens, enfolds, and enriches our lives, if only we open ourselves to Him.

I found this out in a profound way when my husband was diagnosed with leukemia. I never realized how close God could be to me until I needed Him that close. My husband moved to a large city four hours away because the type of treatment he needed was not provided in our area. I worked, and my job provided our health insurance, so we only saw each other for two or three weekends each month. Our two youngest children were still living at home; our youngest was in grade school. So, for nine months, I was both mother and father at home — and a distant caregiver for my husband. When I looked too far out into the future, I wondered if I could make it, and I worried that my husband wouldn't survive. But, as I went through each day, talking, praying, and listening to God, I found that I had just enough strength to get through the day. And, each day, my relationship with God deepened—not because He spent more time with me, but because I opened myself up to Him in a new way. That made all the difference.

Christ tells us that He is the vine, and we are the branches. He gives us clear instructions. He grafts us in, and we bond with Him. This is the first step in living the life you were meant to live. We were designed to live as branches. We draw our life force, our energy, and our support from the vine. We provide strength and support to the other branches—and they to us. But, first, we must bond to the vine, to Christ.

How do we do this?

Christ gives us explicit instructions:

> *"Everyone who calls on the name of the Lord will be saved."*
> Romans 10:13

Jesus gives us two steps to begin the bonding process—believe in Him as our Savior and call upon (depend on) Him. Isn't that exactly what branches do? They depend on the vine for strength, nourishment, water, and support.

So, according to Scripture, the steps for bonding with Christ are:

1. Believe in Him; trust Him.

2. Depend upon Him for all you need, seek His will, and develop your relationship with Him.

A branch that has been cut off from the vine withers and dies; a person who practices Branch Living thrives by accepting the Lord and bonding with Him. If Jesus Christ is not already the Lord of your life, make the commitment. Speak the words from your heart. There is no set formula for this, but if you are having difficulty, here is an example:

Jesus, I have tried to keep you at a safe distance. I have lived on my own terms, even when I knew they were in conflict with what You wanted for me. Today, I am changing all of this. I am surrendering my life to you, knowing that if I trust you, you will lead me to the life I was meant to live. As a result, I will live a life of purpose and fulfillment. I accept you as my Savior, my teacher, my intercessor, and my friend.

Again, there are no set words. Speak from your heart. When you do, your life will change and you will receive several invaluable gifts.

First, you will be given the gift of a Savior, who will be your advocate. We do not live perfect lives, only Christ did — and He stands before God, in our place, taking our sins upon Himself, if we claim this Gift. Through Christ, the gift of heaven as our home is restored to us. We have a home in paradise!

You also will receive the gift of the Holy Spirit. This is a gift that is often misunderstood. The Holy Spirit is the presence of God within us to provide strength and guidance. If you do not feel His presence, don't worry. Part of the Christian walk is realizing the **fact** of your commitment; your feelings will follow.

What is next?

Know that you are unique, and your relationship with Christ is yours alone. Think of your friendships. No two are alike. Likewise, your relationship with Christ is unique. You need to give this new relationship time to grow and mature, and growth can be slow. But, as you continue, you will see an increase in the "fruits" of the Spirit in your own life. These fruits are love, joy, peace, patience, kindness, goodness, faithfulness, and self-control. (See Galatians 5:22-23.) Just as the grapes that grow on a vine start as mere buds, so your faith starts smaller than a mustard seed — but that seed holds within it the promise of growing into a bush so large that birds can build their nests within it (Matthew 13:32). Faith takes time and care to grow. You have to start somewhere — and now you have!

Next, find a church. This is the "C" in our Branch Living. We will discuss this in greater depth when we get to chapter five. For now, I will only comment that the Christian life is meant to be lived out in community with other followers of Christ. We are stronger when we are together, supporting each other. And just as no family is "perfect," no church is completely harmonious or without flaws. But, God loves the church and wants us to have that fellowship and support in our lives.

In addition to finding your church family, there are other steps you can take to strengthen this bond in Christ. These are often referred to as the "spiritual disciplines." These disciplines will deepen your knowledge and love of God, help you hear His voice, and make your life much richer.

The disciplines can be employed on a daily or periodic basis. As is true for all relationships, strengthening our bond with Christ requires time and commitment. Spiritual disciplines or exercises help us understand our dependence on God. They help us open ourselves to God and receive what He has for us. They strengthen us. They help us hear His voice.

> *"...train yourselves to be godly."*
> 1 Timothy 4:7

This first step in Branch Living—bonding with Christ—is foundational. None of the other steps has the power for success without this bond with Christ.

There are two spiritual disciplines that you should incorporate daily: these are prayer and Bible study. We will discuss each of these separately.

Prayer

There is no better example of a life steeped in prayer than Christ Himself. Over and over, we see that He went off by Himself to spend time with His Father. He spoke with Him regularly. He opened Himself to the intimacy of this relationship, and from it, He derived His strength.

Christ is the vine, planted in the richness of the love of the Father. He lived His life on this earth steeped in that relationship – in that love. God is the owner of field, the gardener, the planter and pruner of the vines. When Christ died, He came back to the earth for a brief period of time to show His disciples that, through Him, there is life after death. He returned to heaven, but sent the Holy Spirit to live in those who believe in Christ. The Holy Spirit nourishes us – He is the presence of God within those who believe. The Spirit serves as a guide, a conscience, for us – but the role the Spirit plays is far more than that:

"In the same way, the Spirit helps us in our weakness. We do not know what we ought to pray for, but the Spirit himself intercedes for us through wordless groans."
Romans 8:26

The Spirit lives within us when we bond with Christ. He serves as the living water, strengthening us, interceding for us, even helping us pray to God when we cannot find the right words. Prayer strengthens our bond with Christ. It keeps the flow between Christ and us open. Here are just a few things the Bible tells us about prayer:

"This is the confidence we have in approaching God: that if we ask anything according to his will, he hears us."
1 John 5:14

"Rejoice always, pray continually, give thanks in all circumstances; for this is God's will for you in Christ Jesus."
1 Thessalonians 5: 16-18

"But to you who are listening I say: Love your enemies, do good to those who hate you, bless those who curse you, pray for those who mistreat you."
Luke 6:27

There is much more that can be said on the subject of prayer. For now, remember, prayer helps strengthen our bond to Christ. It is a privilege to have this access to Him. Pray sincerely, regularly, and from the heart.

I have found prayer very freeing. Unlike speaking with family, friends, or coworkers, I don't have to wait for the right time to speak with God. There are times I have awakened in the middle of the night and have found a few moments of prayer to be calming.

A unique aspect of our relationship with God is that nothing we tell Him will shock Him or make Him care less about us. He already knows what we are doing and what we are thinking. So, we do not need to hesitate to come to him. We come freely!

When I think I don't have time for prayer, I remember Christ. I remember how He completed His entire ministry in just three short years. If anyone could have claimed He didn't have time for prayer, it would have been Him. Yet, He was in constant prayer with His Father. When I look at His example, it drives me to my knees.

This is another key aspect of prayer. It "washes away the soul's imperfections," as St. Francis de Sales wrote. A minister I know recently said that as he gets older, he realizes with greater clarity how sinful his nature really is and how much he needs a savior. Often, we push away thoughts of things we wish we had done but didn't, or things we said but shouldn't have. Prayer and confession help us wash these transgressions out of our lives so we can start afresh.

And, as we pray, our prayer life will grow and mature:

"I used to pray that God would feed the hungry, or do this or that, but now I pray that He will guide me to do whatever I'm supposed to do, what I can do. I used to pray for answers, but now I'm praying for strength. I used to believe that prayer changes things, but now I know that prayer changes us and we change things." Mother Teresa

Prayer does change us. It strengthens us. It calms us. And, that calm strength allows us to dive in and help others.

Remember: Pray often, pray fervently. Do not let a day pass without time spent in prayer. Even better, pray continuously throughout the day for strength, compassion, good judgment, and to know what God wills for you. Pray for those you meet. Pray for situations at hand. Pray.

Bible Study

A second lesson we learn from the life of Christ is how He knew the Scriptures, meditated on them, quoted them, lived them, shared them, and fulfilled them. They were a part of His very being. The disciples, likewise, knew the Scriptures. Jesus frequently said to His disciples, "As you have heard" or "As it is written." As Tim Keller states in one of his sermons, when Christ was on the cross, He "bled Scripture," as over and over he quoted it.

We are blessed to be alive at a time when we can read the Bible in our own language. We can own our own Bibles—and have access to different translations to better understand the meaning behind the words. And yet, because Bibles are so readily accessible, we often take them for granted. Foolishly, we don't take advantage of the greatest treasure we possess.

Reading the Bible, taking it into your heart and living it out in obedience, is the best way to know God. It is "God-breathed." Paul tells us that we should read the Bible because it "is useful for teaching, rebuking, correcting, and training in righteousness." (2 Timothy 3:16). Jesus is our example, and if He managed the ups and downs of this world by steeping Himself in Scripture, shouldn't we?

Often, when I read the Bible, I find something in God's Word with which I don't fully agree. Something that "pushes back" on my beliefs. I have learned that this represents a good opportunity to dig deeper into God's word. God challenges us through His word. A god who didn't challenge us wouldn't be the true God.

Dig deep into each verse. Dr. Keller provides an interesting way to study Scripture. It is a method someone taught him early in his career. Read one verse of Scripture. Look at each word in the verse. What would the verse lose if you removed even one word from it? Write down your thoughts. Reflect on them for 15 minutes or more. When you have finished, circle the one or two words, ideas, or concepts that seem to be most important to you within that verse. Then meditate upon them throughout your day.

People who aspire to excellence know that they need to have a compass, a sense of direction, outside of themselves to guide them. They need to mold their beliefs and lives to a true standard. And, there is no better, time-tested truth than the Bible. You know people, as I do, who just don't seem to have any core beliefs. They seem to adjust their views and their lives to whatever is popular at that time. This results in confusion and unhappiness.

An exercise that I work through every few years is to write my own personal mission and values statements (for good guidance, see Andy Andrews' blog on Writing Your Own Personal Mission Statement). I write them out, and then come back to them from time to time to see if they still represent my inner core and to ensure that they are in line with God's word. We need to know the truth for our lives. We need to have a high standard we can target and reach. We need a loving and forgiving God when we fail.

What we don't need is to be the umpire for our own lives or for the lives of others. We aren't qualified. We need a "true north" point—and no human on this earth is qualified to set this standard. Only our Maker, who defined the rules and put them into place for our protection, can explain them to us and teach us The Way. Rely on human rules, and we will be a spinning top— because people are forever changing while God always remains the same. It is true that God is still speaking, but He never contradicts what He proclaimed in the Scriptures.

If you attend a church that teaches that God "evolves" and teaches new things, or that our generation is the first to truly understand what God says or means, I would urge you to prayerfully consider attending a different church. God is the same— yesterday, today, and tomorrow. God does not "evolve." He stands outside of time—He always was, is, and will be. He calls

Himself, "I Am." As we grow deeper in Him, our understanding of Him will deepen, but it should never conflict with Scripture.

So, what happens when you read a section of the Bible that you don't understand or with which you disagree? First take it to Christ in prayer and ask Him to help you understand it. Next, take it to a wise preacher, friend, or colleague whose life and "light" reflect Christ. Ask that person to help you understand what you have read. And, turn to theologians. I study only one chapter of the Bible each day, but I read commentaries by three different Bible scholars along with the passage.

Yes, pray, pray, pray for wisdom and understanding. But, keep in mind the Bible's warning:

> *"For the time will come when people will not put up with sound doctrine. Instead, to suit their own desires, they will gather around them a great number of teachers to say what their itching ears want to hear"*
> 2 Timothy 4:3

You always can find scholars who will tell you that what you hope is true. There are ministers, priests, and spiritual advisers who will tell you that the wrong you are doing is right. Or worse, that there is no wrong, only "learning experiences." If you study history, you soon find that there is nothing taking place in our society that didn't take place in ancient cultures as well.

> *"What has been will be again, what has been done will be done again; there is nothing new under the sun."*
> Ecclesiastes 1:9

So turn to the Bible; let it fill you heart. Memorize scripture, especially those passages that speak to you in a powerful way. Remember, we read the Bible not only to deepen our intellectual understanding—but also to give God the means to change the trajectory of our lives.

"You have died with Christ, and he has set you free from the spiritual powers of this world. So why do you keep on following the rules of the world..."
Colossians 2:20

In addition to prayer and reading the Bible, other disciplines that strengthen your walk with Christ include:

Worship

Fasting

Solitude

Silence

Sabbath Keeping

Personal Reflection

Journaling

Confession

Practicing Simplicity

Serving

Learning

This is not an exhaustive list, and there are many good books on the disciplines Christ followers should bring into their lives. The Bible gives us the ultimate purpose of spiritual disciplines, and that is to "train yourself to be godly." (1 Timothy 4:7)

Donald S. Whitney, in his book, *Spiritual Disciplines for the Christian Life*, notes that the spiritual disciplines help us deepen our faith, and likens this "going deep" to mining for gold.

You can practice these disciplines through support of a small group or on your own. To learn more about the Spiritual

Disciplines, I highly recommend two books: *Spiritual Disciplines for the Christian Life* by Donald Whitney and *The Spirit of the Disciplines* by Dallas Willard.

In summary, bond to Christ and live as a Christ follower by joining a church family, developing an active prayer life, steeping yourself in God's word, and practicing spiritual disciplines.

Now, it's your turn!

At the end of each section of the book, we will address the "Five Ds" necessary for discernment.

They are:

Delve

Discover

Dream

Decide

Do It!

In your journal/ planner, take time now to reflect on this chapter:

1. Delve

- Have you accepted Christ as your Savior?
- Have you found a church family?
- Have you been baptized?
- Do you find time to pray throughout your day?
- Do you find time in your day to read the Bible?
- Do you practice spiritual disciplines?
- How can you incorporate one or more new disciplines into your life?

2. **Discover**

- What stands in your way of taking these steps?
- How can you remove these barriers?
- How can you free space in your day to strengthen your bond with Christ through time spent with Him?
- How can you make this manageable and pleasurable, not another task to add to your busy day?

3. **Dream**

Imagine yourself looking back on your life a year from now. Where do you want to be in your relationship with Christ? What steps should you take that will make you feel that you have made real progress in your relationship with Christ? Write these down and give details.

4. **Decide**

Reflecting on what you wrote regarding your dreams, what actions can you take to achieve them?

Write down your goals for your relationship with Christ this year. Brainstorming is fine—we will refine them in later chapters. Remember to set reasonable goals. If you try to leap too far ahead, you could become discouraged and give up.

What can you commit to doing daily, weekly, monthly to bond more closely with Christ?

5. **Do It!**

Review the goals you established in your "Decide" section. It is time to refine them. See if you have addressed the following suggested areas:

1. Find a church in which you will be taught, led, and supported. If you already belong to a church, how can you use your gifts and talents to expand the outreach or cohesiveness of the church?
2. Develop an active prayer life.

3. Pledge to pray and study Scripture daily (even just for a few minutes.)

4. Begin incorporating other spiritual disciplines in your life.

All of these take so little time and provide tremendous rewards!

In management courses, students are taught to develop SMART goals. The acronym was developed by George T. Doran and presented in the November 1981 issue of *Management Review*. Since that time, the acronym has evolved with many different definitions. Here is one that I use:

SMART goals are:

1. **S**pecific

2. **M**easurable

3. **A**ttainable

4. **R**elevant

5. **T**imely

Turn now to your journal and write one SMART goal for each goal listed in your "Do It" list. Here is an example: I want to find a church home within the next three months. To do this, I will visit a new church every two weeks until I find one that preaches the Gospel, challenges me to grow and serve, and feels like a church family

Here is another **SMART** goal: I will read one chapter of the Bible at least five days each week. I will purchase a commentary to better understand the meaning of what I have read.

Enjoy writing your goals. Don't punish yourself if you miss targets—even for long stretches. Dust yourself off, ask yourself if these are still the things that are important to you, and—if so—Do Them!

Find a Branch Living group for discussion, fun, prayer, and accountability. Visit our webpage. If there isn't a Branch Living group in your area, email us to learn how you can start one (visit BranchLiving.com). Bonding with God is an individual act, but growing in our Christian walk is best done in community. Branch Living groups offer support and fellowship along the way.

Chapter 2

Relationships

We have relationships with many different groups of people: family, friends, church members, people in our communities, and coworkers. Our roles in each of these areas take on different forms at different times. But, our overarching role is to love. Love is the foundation of our relationship with God. Love is the basis of all relationships.

"It is the Holy Spirit's job to convict, God's job to judge, and my job to love."
Billy Graham.

This was one of the most profound and freeing insights I have received from a fellow Christian. And, it is congruent with Scripture. Our task is to share God's love and truth with those around us. We do not have to judge them—in fact, we shouldn't do so, because they are no more or less sinful than we are. We can judge the sin—but not the sinner. That is God's territory. Also, it is not our job to convict the sinner of his sin. That is the job of the Holy Spirit. So what is our job? Love the person. Pray for the person. Do not support the sin, support the person.

Jesus tells us, "'*Love the Lord your God with all your heart and with all your soul and with all your mind.' This is the first and greatest commandment. And the second is like it: 'Love your neighbor as yourself.' All the Law and the Prophets hang on these two commandments.*" Matthew 22: 37-40.

This is the second step in Branch Living—loving those around us. We are told not only to love them, but to love them as we love ourselves.

Jesus also adds a new commandment, "*A new command I give you: Love one another. As I have loved you, so you must love one another. By this everyone will know that you are my disciples, if you love one another.*" John 13:34-35.

I think John Piper states this best:

> The words "*as I have loved you*" contain a **pattern** for our love for each other, and they contain a **power** for our love for each other.

So, in our relationships, we first look for the "pattern" of Jesus' love.

What was that pattern?

> Jesus loved everyone, no matter what his or her position or circumstances.

> Jesus paid particular attention to those who didn't "fit the mold" of society—the tax collectors, prostitutes, Gentiles, etc.

> Jesus approached each relationship as an opportunity to serve in a unique manner, according to the needs of the person at hand.

Jesus surrounded himself with a close group of friends, with whom He shared His heart and, from whom, at times, He asked for support.

Jesus felt responsibility for the welfare of his family, as demonstrated by His care and concern for His mother.

Wow!

Where do we get the strength to do all of that?

The power comes through the vine. It is the only way we, as branches, can do this. Our souls "thirst," and only God can quench this thirst. When we bond with Him, He provides us with a constant source of "Living Water," which is His spirit living within us and counseling us. This is our power. This is our strength.

There is a well-known illustration of this called "The Tale of the Two Seas."

The Sea of Galilee is beautiful. It has blue water and is full of fauna and flora. Trees line its banks where children splash and play. The Jordan River makes this sea, flowing down from the sunny hills. And life is happy and vibrant around this sea.

From the Sea of Galilee, the Jordan River continues to flow south. It flows into another sea, the Dead Sea. Here there are no fish swimming, no birds flying above, no families sunning near the shoreline. The water here is undrinkable. Life does not exist in it.

One might ask: What makes this enormous difference between these neighboring seas? Could it be the Jordan River? No. The same flowing waters empty into both bodies. It is not the soil, not the people, not the geography.

So what is the difference?

The Sea of Galilee receives, but does not keep the waters of the Jordan River. For every drop that flows into it, another drop flows out. The Sea of Galilee gives equally as it receives.

But the Dead Sea keeps the Jordan. It has no outlet. Every drop it gets, it keeps. It does not share. *(Adapted, Source: talkaboutgiving.org)*

Christians liken the Jordan River to the Living Water that Christ gives. Some Christians believe that the Living Water is the Holy Spirit — the Spirit of God who lives in each Christian. Others say it is Jesus, and yet others say it is eternal life. Whatever our interpretation, it is clear that the Living Water is what flows to us when we bond to Christ. It is what our souls need to keep from thirsting. It sustains us. And, it is ever flowing. God intends us to let this living water overflow to those with whom we are in relationship.

First, the bond.

Next, the strength to love those whom God surrounds us with or puts in our path. Without the first step, we do not have the strength to build relationships the way God intended us to.

So let's explore some of these relationships. First, family.

"The world today is upside down because there is so very little love in the home, and in family life. We have no time for each other. Everybody is in such a terrible rush, and so anxious and in the home begins the disruption of the peace of the world."
Mother Teresa

Our family relationships are the only ones we do not choose — therefore they are the most challenging. If you have limited time to invest in relationships, family should come first. As Mother Teresa so eloquently puts it, peace in the world begins with peace and love in the home. Your family members need regular ongoing doses of love and time. These relationships are the bedrock of all other relationships. They contribute to our early development and set a pattern — good or bad — for our future relationships. If you have strong family relationships, you can use this as a strong basis for developing your other relationships. If you come from a dysfunctional family, your relationship with Christ and with other Christians, including Christian counselors, can help you work through any damage that was done so that you can have healthy relationships in the future.

There are individuals in our lives who, for whatever reasons, cannot or choose not to control their impulses to be cruel, insulting, or controlling. God requires us to forgive them, love them, and pray for them. However, God never requires us to bring those who are nasty, demeaning, or abusive into our intimate circle. If they seek true reconciliation, then we are obliged to reconcile. God requires us to love every person; we do not have to like how they behave.

This is another very valuable lesson I learned later in life. Someone once said that when we do not forgive someone it is like drinking poison and expecting the other person to die. I drank a lot of poison until I realized this truth. Now I try to make forgiveness a habit. I want to "travel light," so why carry all of this around? I turn it over to God, and move on.

> *"A happy marriage is the union of two good forgivers."*
> Ruth Bell Graham

By the Holy Spirit, Christ helps us learn how to truly forgive so that the pain of the past no longer haunts us. We remember it, but it no longer defines us.

Next, let's consider our relationships with our friends. My son's minister once preached a sermon that stuck with me. He noted that friendship is one of the least compelling relationships in our lives. We tend to put all other relationships — out of love or duty — ahead of our friendships. He stated that they are the least valued, but are some of the most important relationships we can have.

Real friends are rare gems — and just as families take love and time, so do our friendships. Truly close friendships are few, because we do not have time for many. So, what can we do?

First, we must **pray** for true friendships.

Second, we must **make ourselves available** to friends in terms of time, place, and attitude.

We need to **free up time** for friendships to develop; we must free up space in our schedules.

Next, we need to **spend time in the places** where friendships can form.

What C.S. Lewis believed — and stated throughout much of his writing — is that unlike lovers who gaze at each other, friends look at or toward something. Friendship is often rooted in common projects, goals, and beliefs. So, to have a better chance of finding friends, we should go to places where people are actively taking part in something about which we are passionate. This could mean working at an animal shelter, volunteering for a political cause, or taking part in a knitting group. But, most especially, it can mean spending time at church, where we "worship a common Lord." So, to find true friends, we must look into ourselves, find our passions, and seek kindred people. When we do these things, we dramatically increase our likelihood of finding friends.

Once we have friends, we should, as Jennie Jerome Churchill said, treat them "as you do your pictures, and place them in their best light." See the best in them. Encourage them. Help them to shine.

And, friendships flourish when we can lighten up and laugh together. People like to be with others who lighten life's load a bit.

"Good humor is a tonic for mind and body. It is the best antidote for anxiety and depression. It is a business asset. It attracts and keeps friends. It lightens human burdens. It is the direct route to serenity and contentment."
Greenville Kleiser

A third set of relationships that need our attention is our relationships with fellow church members. Some may be our friends, but there may be others whom we don't know well or with whom we feel friction.

Where friction exists, the most important things we can do are to love and to pray for them. These two acts will keep hostility at bay. We should tell ourselves, "This is my family in heaven, for eternity. I need to begin to love and know them here." (Remember, we probably drive them crazy at times also!)

We need to lift up the painful relationships, the hurts, and the heartaches to God. He can mend them. Never give up —keep praying. Do not allow differences to tear apart the body of Christ.

The church should be the training ground for our relationships in the community and at work. Jesus calls us to be "salt" and "light" in the world, which means we need to stand out in terms of our kindness, patience, goodness, and works toward justice and peace. When people encounter us, they should see Jesus working in our lives and want Him in their lives. This is a steep order— and can only occur through the first step in Branch Living— bonding with Christ.

The last point concerning relationships applies to all types of relationships: use words carefully—but use them. When we are angry, hold back—when we are happy and loving, let go.

If we make people feel loved, respected, cared for, and significant, we will have good relationships.

So, let's move to our "Five Ds":

Delve

Discover

Dream

Decide

Do It!

1. **Delve**

Do you show compassion to all of those with whom you come in contact with, including and especially those who do not "fit the mold"?

Do you seek ways to serve those around you in a manner appropriate to their unique desires and needs?

Have you developed a small group of true friends with whom you can share your heart?

Do you seek God as the Source to meet your true needs?

Do you feel responsibility for the welfare of your family? Do you demonstrate this responsibility in real ways?

2. **Discover**

When you answered these questions, where did you find that your relationships fell short?

Are there relationships that need improvement? How so?

Are you lonely for friendship?

Do you seek in others what only God can give you? Do you expect too much from others?

Do you judge those around you as opposed to understanding them?

Are there problems within your family relationships that you should address?

Do you carry guilt concerning any relationships?

Are there relationships that are particularly painful? Those that need deep healing?

Are there people you can turn to for help?

Do you pray for hurt relationships?

3. **Dream**

How would you like the relationships around you to improve? Focus on each area: your family members, your friends, your coworkers, and your church family. Select particular relationships that you most want to develop, mend, and start. List relationships that you don't have but would like to have.

4. **Decide**

Select just a few relationships you want to work on or work toward. Devise a plan. Think of other persons who can help you in these relationships.

5. **Do it!**

Pray that God will help you in setting your relationship goals. Write each down. Remember where you want to be with each of them one year from now: relationships you have--and those you want to have.

Refine them now to SMART goals. Specific~ Measurable~ Attainable ~ Relevant ~ Timely

Example: I will meet with my pastor to discuss how I can overcome the hurt feelings I have with my sister. I will work with him to devise a plan within the next month.

Example: I will attend one class at the community college in an area I want to explore. I will do this by September.

Example: I will volunteer at the local animal shelter by May. In this way, I expand my opportunity to meet people who share my passion for animals.

Example: I will form a Branch Living group at my church and invite those who want to improve their lives to share this journey with me. I will speak to my minister about this by the end of February.

Example: I will have a date night with my husband once each month. I will sit down with him in the next two weeks to schedule the dates for the rest of the year. I will arrange for babysitters by the end of the month.

It's your turn! Go for it!

Chapter 3

Almsgiving

Giving. It is an act that every world religion requires or promotes.

Giving is one way we "out flow." We discussed our abundance of living water from the Spirit, and what happens when the living water is bottlenecked and cannot flow. "Alms," or giving, is what we naturally do as Christians—it keeps our currents going. It is our "flow."

Why do we give?

We are made in God's image, and He is the ultimate Giver. He gave us life, love, and all good parts of our lives. He made it all— He gives it all. He gave us His Son. His Son gave us life by giving up His own life. The Bible is many things, but at the forefront, it is a love story of giving.

We are Christ's representatives, and as such, we represent Him to the world. A defining characteristic of Christ is giving—abundantly and without counting the cost.

We were made to give. We simply cannot be happy by hoarding, though our human nature would tell us otherwise. If we want to be happy, we have to be good givers.

We please God when we give. When we give, we are serving Him well.

What should we give?

We must give of ourselves. Generally speaking, this means we must give one of three things—or all three: some of our time, talents, and treasures. But that is not all: we must also give away our heart. That is what Jesus did. John writes, "We love because He first loved us." (1 John 4:19)

> *"The only gift is a portion of thyself."*
> Ralph Waldo Emerson

> *"Freely you have received; freely give."*
> Matthew 10:8

First, let's look at time.

You can give the gift of a moment—or the gift of many years. The gift of a moment can be as simple but day changing as a smile or a friendly greeting that is heartfelt. You look into a person's eyes—you make the connection. And then you smile from your heart to theirs.

> *"Kindness has converted more sinners than zeal, eloquence, or learning."*
> Fredrick W. Faber

It is easy to give this gift to many people throughout the day—to strangers as well as those you know well.

A larger gift of time — perhaps the most important gift you give — is prayer. Prayer is our ongoing communication with God. We pray directly to Him. We ask others to pray for us or with us. Prayer matters!

> *"More things are wrought by prayer than this world dreams of."*
> Albert Lord Tennyson

In 1 Thessalonians 5:17, we are told to "pray continually." All day long, we pray for those around us — their needs, their concerns, their fears, and their hopes.

Up to now, we have considered small gifts of time. Now, we turn to large ones such as visiting the shut-ins, running errands for the homebound or spending time with those who are lonely.

> *"The true measure of a man is how he treats someone who can do him absolutely no good."*
> Samuel Johnson

> *"Don't judge each day by the harvest you reap but by the seeds you plant."*
> Robert Louis Stevenson

The source of our giving should be the love we feel for God and for others. Even if we do not feel love for those to whom we give, we should demonstrate love to them because they are created in the image of God and because God loves them. And, feeling follows action. If we do the loving thing for someone, we might, over time, begin to warm toward him or her.

> *"Truly, I tell you, whatever you did not do for one of the least of these, you did not do for me."*
> Matthew 25:45

> *"Loneliness and the feeling of being unwanted is the most terrible poverty."*
> Mother Teresa

Think of the many ways you can give your time that will make a difference. So often, we think we don't have the time, but when we push ourselves to make the time, we find we have all the time we need.

"My faith demands – this is not optional – my faith demands that I do whatever I can, wherever I am, whenever I can, for as long as I can with whatever I have to try to make a difference."
Jimmy Carter

We have explored the needs our family, friends, and loved ones have of our time. The biggest lesson I have learned regarding time is to not hold too tightly to my plans—people's needs often take priority over my carefully planned day—and that is as it should be.

"The measure of a life, after all, is not its duration but its donation."
Corrie ten Boom

We must also give of our talents. Each of us has been given unique gifts for one purpose—to share them! Whether you can teach, coach, encourage, lead—whatever your gifts, use them to serve others. Your talents and gifts were given to you to give away!

Moving beyond time and talents, we must give of our money. Scripture challenges us to give at least ten percent of our income to God. This includes through the church and to those in need. If we aren't meeting that threshold yet, we must work toward it. If we are at this level of giving, we should push ourselves to give a bit more.

If we already give ten percent of our money to our church and other causes, we should try giving ten percent to the church and additional money to other causes.

It is important to ask ourselves every now and then, "Whose resources—time, money, possessions—are these?" When we remind ourselves that everything we have, everything we possess, belongs to God, and that we take nothing with us when we leave this life, it becomes even easier to give. Heaven will be filled with good givers who serve others and receive joy each day from the gift of giving.

How do we give?

I once heard a wealthy man say that he at one time struggled to tithe, but as his wealth increased, his goal became to live on a tithe, and give the other 90% away. Another man stated that he knew how much to give because his goal was to give until it "hurt." If the giving wasn't impacting his life or his wealth, he felt he clearly was not giving enough.

Tim Keller puts Christians and wealth into a perspective I had never considered. He noted in a sermon that it is important for Christians to be represented in all of the income brackets so their influence can impact all levels of society. But, he also suggests that whatever income bracket Christians might be in, they should live in the lower tier of that income grouping, so that they can represent Christ as good givers, and not be stressed by financial concerns.

Jesus gives us guidance on our need to give, no matter what our income, through a parable:

> As Jesus looked up, he saw the rich putting their gifts into the temple treasury. He also saw a poor widow put in two very small copper coins. 'Truly I tell you,' he said, 'this poor widow has put in more than all the others. All these people gave their gifts out of their wealth; but she out of her poverty put in all that she had to live on.'
> Luke 21: 1-4

Everyone benefits through giving—and the good giver benefits most.

Whatever we give, we are instructed by God to give in such a manner that our gifts are between Him and us.

> Be careful not to practice your righteousness in front of others to be seen by them. If you do, you will have no reward from your Father in heaven.
> Matthew 6:1

To summarize:

Give freely.

Give with love.

Give with compassion.

Give intentionally.

Give quietly.

When I see someone in need who seems unapproachable, I remind myself that this is someone's child, someone's sister, a child of God — a person deserving of my best. Jesus calls us to get involved in the lives of those in need. We are to follow his example of redeeming and renewing our world over and over. It is a lifelong calling for all children of God.

Another way to think of this is as "coming alongside" those in need, and not just handing out money. There are groups that work to empower those in communities with tremendous needs to solve their own problems. They ascribe to the philosophy expressed in the ancient Khmer proverb, "Only a spider can repair its own web." More and more, I read articles by persons who live in community with the poor and disadvantaged who urge Christians not to "drop" into countries for mission trips, to fix a building and then leave. They say that these sudden in-and-out trips, or sudden infusions of cash, disrupt the community and do not create lasting change. Our intentions may be good, but our actions do not achieve what we seek to accomplish. So, more and more, I am trying to help bring about real and lasting change by giving to ministries which are operating in the communities needing help.

We must be smart about our giving! We should not give just for the sake of giving and waste God's precious resources. We should investigate the charities we want to help. The Internet has a wealth of sites that rate charities as to what percentage of the gifts they receive actually is used to help those they profess to help.

My son, who lives in New York City, has taught me is to always be prepared to give effectively. When I gave cash to those who approached me on the streets, he told me that I was enabling them to stay in a desperate lifestyle. Rather than hand out cash, he said, I should give my money to those who worked with the homeless. Or, if I felt compelled to give directly to those in need, I should purchase gift cards to restaurants in the area that didn't serve alcohol, and hand those out, so that the person could have a good meal. Sometimes we really do have to examine whether our giving is helping us feel good and if it really is making the difference we seek to make.

Lastly, we must give with gratitude!

We should never forget how blessed we are—and what a blessing it is to serve those in need. When you give, say a little prayer, "God, thank you for blessing me so abundantly. Please let me serve as a conduit through which your riches and blessings can flow to others."

Delve

Discover

Dream

Decide

Do It!

1. **Delve**

Do you pray for those around you?

Do you give your time to those in need to those with whom you have relationships?

Do you give of your earnings?

In each of these cases, do you give until it impacts your standard of living?

2. Discover

When you answered these questions, in what ways did it seem that your giving falls short?

Think about those around you. What are their needs? How could you address them through giving some of your time, talents, and money?

Do you support charities that touch your heart?

Do you support the church?

3. Dream

Think ahead in the year to come. Imagine yourself looking back on this year. How would you like your giving to have improved? Focus on each area: time, talents, and finances. Where could you improve your giving? What would make you feel like you had truly made a difference?

4. Decide

God permits us to share His love and share His work through giving. List the people, charities, and the church with which you feel you should share your time/ talents/ and money. How much money should you give? How much time can you give? Set reasonable goals, but goals that will make a difference in your life — and in the lives of those to whom you "gift."

5. Do it!

Turn to your journal. Pray that God will help you in setting your almsgiving goals. Write each down. Remember where you want to be with each of them one year from now. Think of your time, your talents and your gifts. How can you best serve others with them?

Set goals for yourself in each area—or list the people, charities, and church you want to support, then list the gift (s) you want to share with each.

Now refine them now to SMART goals. Specific~ Measurable~ Attainable ~ Relevant ~ Timely

Example: I will sponsor a child through Compassion International beginning in April.

Example: I will give my church $___ per week.

Example: I will go to the local nursing home once each month and play the piano for the residents.

Remember, work toward tithing. If you tithe, remember to give not because you are commanded to—but because you want to. Think of small gifts you can give throughout the month so that you are an "active" giver, engaged in doing the work of God on a consistent basis.

I said earlier that giving should cause some "pain" or at least a difference in our lifestyle—we will reap far more than we give. I promise. Giving will give back to you—you will feel the love and the joy of working with God to redeem His world—to set things right.

And, it doesn't get any better than that!

Chapter 4

New or Renew

A Reflection by Cardinal John Henry Newman, 19th Century English theologian and author:

"God created me to do Him some definite service; He has committed some work to me which He has not committed to another. I have my mission – I may never know it in this life, but I shall do His work. Therefore, I shall trust Him. Whatever, wherever I am. I cannot be thrown away. If I am in sickness, my sickness may serve Him; if I am in sorrow, my sorrow may serve Him. He does nothing in vain. He knows what He is about."

We follow the One who makes all things new (Revelations 21:5). Jesus healed the leper. He gave sight to the blind. He freed the sinner from the heavy weight of sin. He raised the dead. And, if we permit Him to work in our lives, He can form us into the people He envisioned us to be from the very start.

Life is hard. We all get bruised and a bit battered on the way. We collect bad feelings, bad habits, bad attitudes, and they influence the way we live our lives, who we hang out with, what happens to our dreams and goals.

There is only One who can help us clear the garbage from our lives and use the hurts and pains to help us grow. Only One who can help us take these lessons and help – not hurt—others. There is only One who can take the pain on Himself and give us restored lives. That One is Jesus Christ.

So, how does this work?

First, we must invite Him into our lives—our hearts—and commit our lives to Him. I spoke about this in an earlier chapter, but it is a key step. Christ will help us become new persons, but He will not force Himself into our lives.

Next, once we invite Him in, we must spend time with Him, developing our relationship with Him as He does His work in and through us. This is a lifetime commitment, but it also is a lifetime adventure. God will continually work to make us the people He intended us to be. Just as plants grow at an imperceptible rate, so it is with our spiritual growth. We work with Jesus to "clean house," and we find ourselves eventually saying, "You know, I am no longer bothered by that problem" or "I no longer feel anger toward that person." Such things generally do not happen overnight.

So, once we invite Christ into our lives, how does this spiritual growth occur? We grow as our relationship with and commitment to Christ grow.

Think about the relationships we have with others. How do they grow? We grow closer with friends and family members through 1. Spending time together, 2. Communicating with each other, 3. Getting to know each other, 4. Being there for each other.

It's the same way in our relationship with Christ. Here are some ways we can grow in our intimacy with Him:

1. Spending time alone with Him in prayer and meditation – speaking to Him and listening to Him.

2. Reading Scripture – so that He can speak to us through His word. Preferably, read the Bible with a reliable commentary in order to better understand the context and the language in which it was written. As the pastors of Blackhawk Church in Middleton Wisconsin often state, "The Bible was not written to us but for us."

3. Attending worship—Praying with other believers. Getting to know your family in Christ! Confessing sins. Taking Communion.

This is a lifelong process – this side of heaven, we can never know Christ completely. We always can learn more. Grow more. Discover more about Him.

To make new and to renew has two components: setting goals on how to work with God to improve ourselves: our attitudes, physical health, habits, etc. and how to work with God to renew/ make new the world around us.

In focusing on our own individual needs for renewal or to be made new, we must give serious consideration to bad habits, attitudes, patterns of spending our time and money, and ways we treat others. How would we like to change? How can we better reflect God? How can we improve our health/ our strength to reflect that our bodies are the temples of God?

But, "newness" isn't just about us. God calls us to work with Him to make all things new: our relationships, our community, our world. Let's examine each of these.

Relationships – In the relationships section of this book, we discussed the calling we have to love our neighbors – those with whom we are in relationship – and how we must work with Him to heal torn relationships, knowing that often this takes time and divine intervention. It takes two people to make a relationship, and we cannot control what takes place on the other side. For that, we must pray and turn matters over to God. But, we can control our side of the relationship. We can be loving, caring, and compassionate. When God fills us with His love, when we know how much He cares about us, we can treat others with kindness no matter how they treat us. How? Because our cup is already brim full!

Our Community/Our world - In the opening quote of this chapter, Cardinal Newman states that we were all created by God to play a particular role in His ultimate plan—and we may not realize what our role was until we have finished this life. But, we have a role to play—and the best way for us to realize our role is to develop our relationship with Christ, explore and understand the gifts we have been given by God, and to use those gifts to the best of our ability to bring others to Him. We let others see His work in us, His life in us, and reflect the good that is within Him, so they, too, will desire to know Him.

If you believe that you are not on the right course, that you are not in sync with God and that you need to get back on track, it is never too late. The fact that you are still breathing—still here on this earth—means that God still believes you have a role to play in some way. I am a minister's wife, and I have seen truly miraculous life changes occur with people even in their 80s and 90s because they felt compelled to change. You can't undo the past, but you can turn a corner and create a brighter future.

It is not easy to get out of a rut. It is not comfortable to try to begin again—or to make even small modifications in our lives to be closer to God's will. But this is the only true path to happiness and to fulfillment. The world will not tell you this—but God does.

> *"Blessed is the one who does not walk in step with the wicked*
> *or stand in the way that sinners take*
> *or sit in the company of mockers,*
> *but whose delight is in the law of the Lord,*
> *and who meditates on his law day and night.*
> *That person is like a tree planted by streams of water*
> *which yields its fruit in season*
> *and whose leaf does not wither —*
> *whatever they do prospers.*
> *Not so the wicked!*

They are like chaff
That the wind blows away.
Psalm 1: 1-4

If we root ourselves in Jesus and study God's words and His ways, we are promised that we will "yield fruit in season," our contributions will not "wither" and we will "prosper." The world simply cannot offer a better plan!

If we are on the path that God has selected for us, we still need to refine our walk day by day, becoming new and renewed.

We all get into ruts. We live our lives in certain patterns and ignore the new growth that is around us and inside of us. We forget that we must always be in a process of growth and renewal. As long as we have breath, we have purpose.

So, how do we know our purpose—our part to play in God's design? How do we know our part in making "all things new" –in introducing others to Christ?

One of the first and most difficult parts of this is realizing that the focus is not on us. The world will tell us that we become happier and more satisfied if we turn our focus on ourselves, that the void we feel inside can be best satisfied if we keep trying to fill our own needs, wants, and desires. But, focusing on ourselves or asking the world to focus on us cannot fill this void. It can only be filled by serving others.

That is the secret to happiness—it is the secret to finding our purpose. We must discover the gifts that God has given us to love others in our own special way, to help guide them to Him, to help guide them "home." It is why we are here. It is how we find fulfillment and purpose. And, the world will never tell you this—ever. The lie that the world tells you is that you must focus on yourself to find happiness. God says, "Let me focus on you. Let me love you. You go forward—boldly—and do what you were brought here to do to further my kingdom."

So how do we do this?

One of the most helpful tools I have used is a spiritual gift analysis. Spiritual gifts are not natural talents or a specialty ministry. Spiritual gifts are tools for building the church (body). They are a divine calling with a divine responsibility.

You answer a series of questions and then see where you rank in terms of "strength" for each of the gift categories: evangelism, teaching, showing mercy, serving, giving, administration, etc. I found that my top gifts are in administration, pastoring or shepherding, and exhortation (encouraging, advising, motivating). And that felt so right. I have worked in management for more than 25 years. I have used my "pastoring" or "shepherding" skills in my professional role and have also used these gifts in many other ways. I taught Sunday school for 24 years, served as an assistant Boy Scout troop leader, and led several civic and social organizations. I love to encourage and motivate others to reach goals or milestones (exhortation). It is why I am writing this book—to encourage you to release your gifts and thereby help renew this wonderful world.

There are many types of spiritual gift assessments. Find the one that best suits you. The survey results aren't meant to box you in but rather to help guide you to realize the gifts that you have—the tools you have been given to help build the fellowship of Christ followers. Trust me, when you find the right guidance, you will have this wonderful "aha" moment.

But, knowing your spiritual gifts isn't all you need to discern the part you have been given in renewing the world around you. Sometimes, you have to try new ministries, serve in new ways, to see if what you are doing is a good fit.

But, now is your time. Get started!!

"The mass of men lead lives of quiet desperation and go to the grave with the song still in them."
Henry David Thoreau

Don't let that happen to you. Push forward. It may be that you only realize your gifts in hindsight. But keep moving forward.

You walk. God will steer and you will find you are on the right path.

Another way to determine if the path you seek to follow is part of God's plan for your life is to do the three-way test:

1. Do you see confirmation in Scripture for your desires? Or, is there anything in Scripture that would give you pause in taking this new path?

2. Do you have a "calling" to take on this new venture? Are you praying about this new course? Do you feel at peace with this new path?

3. Do you see confirmation to take this path from events/ conversations in your life? Do things seem to be naturally moving in this direction?

Although these three tests do not guarantee that the path you have chosen is the correct, God-given path for you, they do direct your thinking in a way to look at many angles of the decision you are facing.

So, how do you use to your spiritual gifts in a new way—or in a way to help renew the church?

Let's walk through the steps we've discussed:

Bond with Christ

Discover your spiritual gifts, through reflection, time, tools, and discussions with other Christians.

Determine how you can use these gifts to further God's kingdom on earth. What can be made new or be renewed? How can your work bring others to Christ?

Remember, the use of your gift or gifts does not need to be confined strictly to the church in the sense of the church building. The Church (God's followers) is everywhere! If you enjoy working with the elderly, volunteer to read a newspaper to nursing home residents or lead a craft or game at the senior center.

Do you enjoy working with animals? Local shelters can always use help. Or do you have a gift for raising money? Organize a group to help!

Is your gift in showing mercy and compassion? Perhaps you could work with a church group on helping women in a homeless shelter, or serving as a Big Brother or Big Sister to a child in need.

In the early days of the church, one of the things that attracted pagans to the church was the visible ways the early Christians cared for one another and for those around them.

In A.S. 125, Aristides, an early Christian philosopher, wrote (about the early Christians):

> *"They walk in all humility and kindness, and falsehood is not found among them, and they love one another. They despise not the widow, and grieve not the orphan. He that hast distributeth liberally to him that hath not. If they see a stranger, they bring him under their roof, and rejoice over him as if he were their own brother: for they call themselves brethren, not after the flesh, but after the Spirit of God; but when one of their poor passes away from the world, and any of them see him, he provides for his burial according to his ability; and if they hear that any of their number is imprisoned or oppressed for the name of their Messiah, all of them provide for his needs....*
>
> *And, if there is among them a man that is needy and poor, and they have not an abundance of necessaries, they fast two or three day that they may supply the needy with their necessary food."*

No wonder the early church was on fire! The Holy Spirit empowered Christians to do God's work on a daily basis. The Holy Spirit empowers us to do the same today.

Our minister recently told a story that he had read online. It concerned a Puerto Rican woman who came to the United States and wanted to serve God at the church. She spoke little English. She and her minister tried to discern what gifts and talents she had that she could use. She spoke of her love of children, and the minister thought she could share her gift by riding the church bus that picked up children for Sunday School—just being there for them.

She did this frequently and let the children know that she loved them—and so did Jesus. This was her gift and her ministry. One of the little boys she had held and spoke to came from an abusive home. She was not aware of this, but she felt called to hold him on her lap and let him know that he was loved. One day he did not get on the bus. She later found out that the child had been beaten to death by his mother the previous Sunday afternoon. She then realized that she had been one of the last—and perhaps only—people to share her love and the love of God with this little boy. Imagine the difference she made to him. Imagine the gift that would have stayed wrapped up had she not followed her desire to serve in the church. Truly, we never know how God will use us until we open ourselves to Him.

There are many needs we can help meet, and through serving others, lead people to Christ.

As we help others, we too are served. Our gifts are refreshed and renewed.

Up to this point, when speaking of becoming new and serving others, we have focused on serving outside of our current vocations. But, you also will find that you will become more interested, more content, and more satisfied in your job if you find within it ways to serve Christ. This does not have to be through sharing Bible verses and prayers (though it might be). It can occur by the care and dedication you show to your work, the fulfillment you find in it as you go through the day working not for your boss or the organization—but for Christ. You renew your spirit toward your job by truly seeing it as a place to employ your gifts.

You hear of these stories more and more: individuals who choose to see the work they do as their ministry—and who change people's lives while doing the work of housekeepers, garbage truck drivers, CEOs, teachers — really any profession. Change your outlook. Change your focus on the work you do. Change people's lives. Change the world.

It may be that as you better understand your gifts, and as you find fulfillment in using them to serve others in venues outside of the workplace, you might find a real love — a true passion — for an entirely new career. You may work with the elderly and decide you want to work as an activity coordinator in a nursing home. You might enjoy entertaining children and decide to become a professional clown! You might help with the church newsletter or website and decide to enter the field of marketing.

Exercising your spiritual gifts, even in small ways, can spark interests for new passions and careers. God can use our small steps to lead us to take big steps we had never imagined possible.

Delve

Discover

Dream

Decide

Do It!

In your journal, take time now to reflect:

1. **Delve**

Renewing Yourself:

Do you spend time alone with Christ?

Do you make a regular practice of reading and studying your Bible to better understand the God we serve?

Do you attend a church and a small group to develop a circle of friends who will challenge you, support you, and help you grow?

Renewing Relationships:

Are there relationships you need to renew or form?

Are there ways you can bring new life to your relationships?

Renewing Your Community/ the World:

Do you know your spiritual gifts?

Have you tried to develop an understanding of your gifts by serving in different ways?

Do you see your job/ profession as a way of serving Christ?

When you see your job/ profession in this light, are there ways you can serve Christ better at work and find new joy in working for Christ?

What attitudes or habits would I like to develop or break to be healthier, happier, and a better reflection of Christ?

2. Discover

When you answered these questions, what did you discover?

If you could serve Christ in any way, what would you like to do?

Think about those around you. What are their needs? How could you address them through your gifts and talents?

What are the areas in you that need to be renewed or made new?

Where is healing needed?

In the broken areas of your community, where do you feel drawn to help?

3. **Dream**

Think ahead in the year to come. Imagine yourself looking back on this year. How would you like your relationship with Christ to be new or renewed? How would you like to work with Christ to make yourself new? What relationships do you need to improve? What areas of your community do you want to help to renew? How do you want to make a difference?

4. **Decide**

God calls on us to be new beings in Christ. What specific areas do you want to ask Christ to help you improve on in the coming year? How do you want to help your community? What gifts can you use to renew the world around you? The key here is to explore how you would like to be "new" and how you would like to contribute to renewing the world around you.

5. **Do It!**

Turn to your journal now and write one SMART goal for each of these areas. Remember, SMART goals are

1. Specific – they state what you will do.

2. Measurable – by how much?

3. Attainable – within your power to achieve (always good to stretch – but you must be able to achieve these goals)

4. Relevant – match your vision for your future.

5. Timely – by when?

Here is an example:

I will work to renew my community by soliciting others to form a group with me to pick up trash in our neighborhood twice each year.

Here are other examples:

In the next eight weeks, I will complete a spiritual gifts assessment to help guide me in my discovery of my spiritual gifts.

I will ask God to help me remove from my life the bad habit I have of gossiping. I will write down each time I find myself repeating this behavior.

I will work to mend relationships with my neighbor by spending time visiting with her each month.

I will use my gift of teaching to help renew my church by volunteering to teach a women's study group.

I will focus on being a more appreciative person. I will write down one aspect of my day for which I am grateful.

Chapter 5

Church

"Church attendance is as vital to a disciple as a transfusion of rich, healthy blood is to a sick man."
Dwight L. Moody

"So you are therefore no longer strangers and aliens, but you are fellow citizens with the saints, and are of God's household, having been built on the foundation of the apostles and prophets, Christ Jesus Himself being the corner stone, in whom the whole building, being fitted together, is growing into a holy temple in the Lord"
Ephesians 2:19-20

"Wherever we see the Word of God purely preached and heard, there a church of God exists, even if it swarms with many faults."
John Calvin

Many people give have given up on church. Others have never been to church, unless for a wedding, funeral, or concert. Many churches around the country are closing or are fighting hard to stay alive, as membership numbers continue to decline.

But there is something much deeper taking place: when the Church is in trouble, the body of Christ is suffering. One of the first things I learned early in my Christian walk is that our lives in Christ are meant to be lived out in community. This does not mean that we are each called upon to live in a commune or be part of a religious order—although that calling may come to some. It means that we are meant to walk together with fellow Christians who enable us to live fully and successfully, encouraging us to fully utilize our gifts.

This Branch Living we have been called to involves rooting ourselves in the vine, Jesus Christ (bonding). But, it also involves living with other branches. We don't all have the same gifts. But, when we work together, we have all of the gifts that the Spirit offers in one place. We come bearing our few offerings, but when we put our gifts together with those of other Christians, simply put, we have a banquet of gifts.

When we try to walk with Christ by ourselves, we deprive ourselves of the richness of what other Christians offer. When we remove ourselves from church, we keep ourselves from the fellowship, companionship, and friendship of other believers who can make the walk easier and more joyful. We don't have the interactions—even debates—that help us grow deeper in our faith, strengthen our beliefs or modify them when necessary. We don't have learned individuals who are readily accessible when we have questions or when our choices should be challenged. We don't have the support and deep caring we need when troubles and sorrows come our way.

In other words, when we don't live out our Christian walk in a church, we deprive ourselves, we deprive other Christians, we deprive the Body of Christ, and we deprive our community. Our lives are markedly less rich. When churches lack resources or close, we deprive our community of a place to come to have its needs met, and in the process, to experience the freedom and joy of life lived in Christ.

Before we go any further, let's better understand what a church is, what it is called to be and to do, the essentials to seek in a church, what you get from church, what you give to church, and why it is an essential component of Branch Living.

When Christ lived and walked on this earth, He completed his acts in a physical body. Through His "human" life, He showed us how we should live our lives. Since ascending back to heaven, He has continued His work through those whom He has called and redeemed. The Church (the entirety of believers) now functions as the Body of Christ to show God's love to the world. Individual churches are small components of this Body of Christ. They are subsets of the full body of believers. We come together as a group of Christians in church to get and to give.

The Church is called to be Christ's bride—His heart, His treasure, that which will carry out His works on earth until He returns. The Church's primary duty is to spread the good news -that God sent His Son to earth to die in our place for our sins, so that we can have a renewed and right relationship with Him. As members of a church, we give our gifts to the church to ensure that this work is done

Another primary role of the Church is to create a safety net for those in need. In this way, the Church carries out the ministries that Christ started in His time on earth: healing of the sick, meeting the basic needs of the poor, befriending the lonely/ the outcast, visiting prisoners, and ensuring that those who are marginalized by society are brought into the fold of the church. This is an enormous job, and that is why so many gifts of so many people are needed. The job is impossible unless the Body of Christ takes on the yoke and has the power of the Holy Spirit to enable the workers. So many people in our culture look to government or social service agencies to carry this burden, but although they can certainly help, they cannot possibly meet this challenge. Only God can take away the guilt of sin that burdens all people and often prevents them from starting over. Only the Holy Spirit can provide the power to love our neighbors as much as we love ourselves. Service agencies are needed—but only the Church has the power to get the deep work done.

One essential thing to seek in a church is its commitment to proclaiming the Gospel as it is written and its willingness to challenge our thinking to move us to biblical truth. Many churches today feel they must tell the people in the pews what they want to hear—whether or not it is biblical. It is true that there is often a need for interpretation to translate the languages of the Bible into our language, and to decipher what was meant for a culture versus what is meant to be a timeless standard of morality. But, when it comes to addressing the biblical message to our culture, the Church must stand apart from the current whims and teach us the Truth.

The Church is to our souls what a hospital is to our physical bodies. We would all love to go to the doctor's office and be told that we were in perfect health—no changes in our behaviors needed. But, would we really want to be told that if it were not true? What if we had high blood pressure, diabetes, or were morbidly obese? We need our physicians to tell us the truth and to help us improve our health and move toward wellness. The same thing holds true when it comes to the state of our souls.

We want to hear that the way we are living is spiritually healthy, that God doesn't look at our acts, only at our hearts. But is that true? Do we each get to determine what is true for us spiritually? Do we each get to set our own standards? Do we get to invent God for ourselves? Do we get to create our own rules based on our feelings? If so, the god we are worshipping is our self.

If truth is defined by what we think or believe, what if your neighbor thinks it is fine to take one of your cars if you have two and he has none? What if your neighbor thinks it is fine to borrow your child for a week? No, deep down we know that just as there are rules of living that keep us physically fit, and if we go against them, we suffer, we also know that there are spiritual truths that if

54

violated will cause us to suffer spiritually. There are natural laws and spiritual laws—and our opinions of these basic truths don't influence them. There is absolute "truth" outside of us. So, shouldn't we seek to know it—and apply it to our lives, so that the truth really will set us free?

As Jesus so succinctly tells us, *"If you abide in my word, you are truly my disciples, and you will know the truth, and the truth will set you free."* John 8:31-32

Don't settle for less than the truth. If you are living a life that is contrary to what Scripture teaches, ask God to show you how to make the changes to bring your life back in line, and the steps you need to take to get there. God will wipe the slate clean at your heartfelt confession, the Holy Spirit will give you the power and strength to make the changes, and your fellow Christians, who also have all fallen short of the lives they are called to lead, will envelop you in love and support to help you through these changes.

"But seek first His kingdom and righteousness and all these things shall be added to you." Matthew 6:33.

What are the other essentials of churches?

Opportunities for fellowship and study, a commitment to Mission and giving, a desire to spread the Word of God throughout the community, a healthy respect for differences of opinions without defiling the Word of God, and a heart to serve all those in need. These can be available within both large and small churches—it is more a matter of purpose and heart than of size.

More and more, churches are finding that "small group ministry" is an essential part of the church's overall ministry. Small groups are groups of church members—and sometimes nonchurch members—who gather at times outside of church hours. Small groups help develop deeper relationships among those who participate. The purpose of such groups varies. Some are formed strictly for fellowship. Others focus on Bible study, book discussion, review and discussion of the prior week's sermon, mission and outreach services, or a combination of these. Small groups make intimacy possible. They allow for the personal support, prayers, and time needed to support fellow Christians. Even small churches are beginning to see a need for small groups — because the Sunday worship service just does not offer sufficient personal time for Christians to develop deeper relationships.

What you need to get from church is God's truth; spiritual development; a "safe zone" in which you can express your thoughts, opinions and beliefs; and fellowship, in which you can get to know members of your future heavenly family even better.

Most importantly, we get to worship and praise God in community. God does not need our worship. He is perfect and does not need anything from us. But because He loves us, He is pleased by our worship, just as we are happy when one of our children runs up to us, throws his arms around us, and says, "Mom, I love you!" We were designed to worship and praise something, to look to something to which to give our praise. If that need is not met by God, we will meet it in other ways. We will turn to our jobs, our children, our spouse, our friends — all wonderful aspects of our lives — but not one of these can stand the weight of our need to worship. We all have a very deep need that only God can fill. Worship Him!

"And, let us consider how we may spur one another on toward love and good deeds, not giving up meeting together, as some are in the habit of doing, but encouraging one another — and all the more as you see the Day coming."
Hebrews 10: 24-25

We do this in church because we are in the company of believers, and worship comes naturally to us when we are with others who believe.

What we give to the church are our spiritual gifts, our hands and hearts to serve, and monetary gifts to continue the mission of the church.

What we get back from the church is a hundredfold of what we put into it. We sit in the presence of God with His children. In Holy Communion, we celebrate our full unity with Him. Through shared confession, shared praise, shared prayer, we get "cleansed," centered, renewed, and ready to face the week ahead.

Attending church is an essential part of Branch Living because church brings together all of the other components we have discussed. Church provides a place and a body with which to worship and strengthen our bond to God. It is a place through which we can form and strengthen relationships. It is a center through which our alms can be given—and through which we can become aware of other opportunities for giving. It is a place where we can explore our gifts and find ways to make our world and ourselves "new."

Here's another reason to attend church: Harvard University researchers analyzed data from the Nurses' Health Study, a survey of 74,534 healthy primarily Christian women. At the start of the study in 1992, participants were asked how often they attended church; the researchers then tracked them for 20 years. By 2012, 13,357 of the women had died. After adjusting for other risk factors, it turned out the ones who attended services more than once a week were 33 percent less likely to have died of any cause than those who never went at all. Church strengthens us for life!

So—get started! If you currently don't participate in one—find a church that can become your spiritual family! Take your time— this is a commitment not much different from marriage. The church you decide on should be one that strengthens you, challenges you, and helps you grow. You should be comfortable there—but not so much that you don't grow. Church should offer you the perfect soil for your Branch Living—helping you discover and use your gifts to their fullest!

If you presently are a member of a church, find new ways to strengthen it—so that it can strengthen you and others in this wonderful Branch Living!

Delve

Discover

Dream

Decide

Do It!

In your journal, take time now to reflect:

1. **Delve**

Do you currently belong to a church?

If yes, does it support and yet challenge you?

If no, what is missing?

Are there Christians in your life whom you admire? Where do they go to church?

2. **Discover**

If you belong to a church, how can you strengthen the church so that it might strengthen you/ the other members?

What would improve your church? How can you help make that happen?

If you are not part of a church, what are you seeking in a church? Are there church members with whom you can discuss your desires?

What troubles you about churches? How can you overcome these objections so that you can make a real commitment to help build the church?

3. **Dream**

Describe your ideal church and church family.

If you are a member of a church, how can you work with others to bring some of these desires to fruition?

If you are not a member of a church, would you feel comfortable asking others if these aspects are present in their churches? Would you feel comfortable visiting churches to find one that does support and challenge you?

If not, how can you move beyond your reluctance?

4. **Decide**

Based on the where you dreams took you, what can you commit to doing? Remember to set reasonable goals. If you try to leap ahead, you could become discouraged and stop.

What can you commit to doing to find or help develop a church that will meet, support and challenge its members?

5. **Do It!**

Write your SMART goals for this section!

Here are examples:

If you are not currently a church member:

1. I will review my list of what features are important to me in the church to which I want to commit my membership. I will finalize this list during the next week.

2. I will ask five of my friends/acquaintances who attend church to describe their churches to me. I will do this by the end of the month.

3. I will explore on the Internet five churches I want to visit, reading their belief statements, missions, and service information.

I will visit three of them in person during the next two months (church "dating").

If you are currently a member of a church:

1. I will review my list of ways I can strengthen my church so that it can strengthen me and the other members. I will discuss this list with my pastor within the next two months.

2. I will begin participating in or will work with others to begin "X" (program/ service component) at the church within the next six months.

Give this a great deal of thought! Enjoy writing your goals!

Chapter 6

Habits

Your life is built upon the habits you develop. If your "habit" is to sit in front of the television from the time you come home until you go to bed, you probably will not be very physically fit nor have many friends.

In this section, you will set goals to help you achieve your "Do-its" from the earlier sections of the book: Bonding with God, Relationships, Almsgiving, New/Renew, and Church. You also will set the goals that lead to the outcomes that you want in the other parts of your life that strengthen you and contribute to the overall success of your own Branch Living.

You work with God, through the power of the Holy Spirit within you, to create the life you were designed to live: the life that will bring you happiness, contentment, and fulfillment. But, you must develop the habits that are the building blocks to that life. Creating positive habits of Bible reading, exercising, writing, giving, seeing friends and family members, attending church, volunteering, and getting enough sleep all require the same process—and here it is:

1. Set your goal. Make it SMART—as we discussed in the "Do it" sections in the previous chapters: Specific, Measurable, Attainable, Relevant, and Time-Based.

For example a goal of weight loss might look like this, "I will lose 35 pounds this year. I will do this at the rate of three pounds per month." This goal is specific—35 pounds. It is measurable—the scale will tell me if I am successful. The weight loss is attainable—physicians in general agree that weight loss of 1-2 pounds per week is a healthy rate of weight loss. And, the goal is time-based, with incremental goals along the way.

2. Make a written commitment to yourself and involve someone else, if possible, in your plans. Many experts in setting goals—and achieving them—agree that simply writing the goal down will put you ahead of the pack in achieving that goal. Have a partner you can work with to achieve the goal, and you are even further ahead. One of my friends, who lost more than 80 pounds, took an unflattering photo of herself and posted it on Facebook and told all of her "friends" that she was going to hold herself accountable through regular posts on Facebook. She took off the weight - more than 80 pounds.

3. Set a reasonable pace for achieving your goal. Allow yourself to fail. And, when you do, dust yourself off and start where you left off.

Too often, we don't allow ourselves to fail in areas that are import to us, while we aren't so hard on ourselves when we fail in routine tasks. Think about it. If you burn the toast, you don't say, "Okay, I'll never make toast again." If you kill a houseplant, you don't say, "That's it—no more plants." We all have failures, at least small failures, all of the time. But, when it comes to habits, we smack ourselves silly and stop there—labeling ourselves as failures. The average smoker quits smoking 7-9 times before he is successful. The point here is to set reasonable goals—allow some failure—and get up and start again until you get it right.

4. Emulate successful people. I don't mean culturally popular people—I mean those who have successfully done what you would like to do. Want to lose weight? Speak with, study, learn from those who have lost weight—and kept it off—in health ways. Want to exercise more? Find a former couch potato who revved it up and is now physically fit and active. Learn from that person!

5. Visualize your success. I know this sounds "airy fairy," but it is true that if you can see yourself some place, it is easier to get there. Public speakers frequently employ this technique. They see themselves giving the speech, expressing themselves with great confidence, and see the audience responding warmly.

6. Consider joining a group! If you are energized by having other people with you on the habit-breaking/ habit developing journey, join a group or create a group of like-minded people who want to work at breaking or developing the habit you are seeking to break/ develop. Start a Branch Living group at your church! (More on that to come!)

7. Always remember—it won't always be easy, but it will be worth it!

8. Explore future chapters in this book for good tips on how to develop/ break some of the common habits.

Supplement your faith with a generous provision of moral excellence, and moral excellence with knowledge, and knowledge with self-control, and self-control with patient endurance, and patient endurance with godliness, and godliness with brotherly affection, and brotherly affection with love for everyone."
2 Peter 2-5

To our faith we add:

Moral Excellence

Knowledge

Self Control

Patient Endurance

Godliness

Brotherly Affection

Love for Everyone

All habits reside in one of these areas, and these areas all require Good Habits.

What Goals are included in this final section?

- Habits that you haven't detailed that will support the other key areas: Bonding with God, Relationships, Almsgiving, New/ Renew, and Church.

- Other goals that you have not detailed yet but would benefit your walk:

(Examples)

- Moral Excellence – not swearing, moving away from sinful behaviors

- Knowledge – going back for a degree/ taking a study group, increasing reading

- Self Control – weight loss, exercise, abstaining from drugs/ anger

- Patient Endurance – devoting yourself to a boring job while you are in it, visiting a lonely person, trying to get along with a difficult person

- Godliness – serving more, evangelizing, worship (Christ-like behaviors)

- Brotherly Affection – reaching out to neighbors, being hospitable to fellow Christians
- Love for Everyone – serving at the free clinic, helping someone in need

It is important to realize at this point that there are no hard boundaries between the sections. In our Christian walk, the areas of Bonding with God, Relationships, Almsgiving, New/ Renew, Church and Habits will have some overlap—and that is okay.

Our Christian walk is not neatly divided into categories.

It represents a blend of who we are and what we do.

So, don't worry where the goal "fits". The Habits section is a nice "catch all". This is why it is last.

So write your goals in this section to address Habits and to address those "goals of the heart" that did not fit neatly in another category—or that you just now became aware of, and you need a place to put them.

Delve

Discover

Dream

Decide

Do It!

In your journal, take time now to reflect:

1. **Delve**

What areas of your life do you want to change?

What has stood in your way? Really think this through. Why have you not accomplished what you have wanted to do?

What bad habits do you want to break?

What new habits do you want to develop?

2. **Discover**

Go back over the past chapters. Write down your list of "Do its" by chapter – list out the "Do its" under Bonding, Relationships, Alms, New/Renew and Church. Write down the other goals you have from this chapter – and any other goals that came to mind as you read this chapter, such as goals to be healthier and stronger, which will help you achieve your other goals. Think of what would bring you joy – something that didn't fit under one of the other chapters – if you achieved it within the year.

Rank order these "Do its." Take your time. You are not giving up any of these goals or dreams. You are just setting your path.

Try to balance your list – make sure you have at least one goal from each of the areas and no more than three goals from one area (B-R-A-N-C and other Habits).

3. **Dream**

Look at your list. Then, set it aside and think about what you would truly like to be able to say you accomplished one year from now. Which of the goals, if achieved, would make you feel that it was a year well lived? Put a star next to those that mean the most to you.

4. **Decide**

Based on the where you dreams took you, what can you commit to doing?

Remember, balance is important in Branch Living. You should have at least one goal in each of the five areas: Bonding with God, Relationships, Alms, New/ Renew, and Church. Ideally, you will limit yourself to no more than 8-15 goals in total – and put the rest in the "bank" bringing them out as you accomplish your top goals. Try to always keep one active goal in each area.

Create your list – circle your top goals – make sure you have one in each area – limit them to eight to 15. Bank the rest.

5. **Do It!**

Turn to your journal. Write one goal on each page.

What habits will you need to develop to achieve these goals? Write the habits/ practices you will need to adopt for each. Be specific.

Congratulations! You now have your plan in place—the goals for your new year—and for the new you!

Next: Common Areas of Personal Growth and then, Putting it all together

Chapter 7

Personal Growth Areas

In the previous chapter, we discussed habits and identified areas of our lives to change or improve. In this chapter, we look at common areas that many of us choose to focus on, and we review tips to help achieve those goals.

Weight Loss

I have been on and off diets for 30 years, since my first child was born. Before the birth of my first child, I occasionally had times when I had to diet, but I pretty much kept my weight on an even keel. But, them something happened during my pregnancy. At first, I was so nauseous that I couldn't keep food down. I continued to lose weight, and my doctor kept encouraging me to eat. Well, around month four, I discovered an ice cream store — actually a frozen custard store — that sold frozen custard with any flavoring or topping you wanted. My favorite was vanilla with chocolate chips blended in. I could keep it down, and it became a craving. A daily craving. Even when I could start eating regular food, I still craved frozen custard.

As my pregnancy progressed, and my weight did as well, my doctor cautioned me to slow down on gaining weight. I didn't. By the time my son was born, I had gained 58 pounds. I almost cried when the nurse said my newborn son weighed seven pounds 11 ounces. How was I going to take off all of that weight?

Well, over time, I was able to bring my weight down, but still was ten pounds over my pre-pregnancy weight when I became pregnant with my second child. I didn't gain as much weight when carrying my daughter—but I did carry an additional ten pounds into my third pregnancy. I ended that pregnancy with the stubborn thirty pounds of excess fat that just would not leave my body (although I invited it to over and over). I tried diets—more than I could count—and I would lose weight, but I would gain it all back within months. Finally, when I was in my mid-fifties, I found several tips that, when taken together, helped me drop 20 pounds over two years. I had to do them in combination, and to be honest, I had to write them down and review them each day so that I didn't forget what works for me.

Disclaimer: Although the following tips work for me, no two people are alike. If you plan on incorporating one or more of these tips into your diet, check with your health care provider first for advice. I am not a medical expert by any means!

1. Plan your meals no less than the day before—preferably two or more days beforehand. In this way, you will have what you need on hand and you won't be as tempted to stray from the plan you set for yourself.

    I hate to write down everything I eat, although this is a strategy that has worked for many people. Instead, I decide ahead of time what my meals and snacks will be and I do not vary from them if it is a dieting day. When I am holding my own with my weight, I am not quite this rigid, but if the scale starts to go up, I am right back in diet mode.

I limit my calories when I am dieting, and I estimate the calorie count in each of my meals and my snacks. I am not rigid in my calorie counting—but I try to keep the count as low as I can while staying full.

2. Prepackage as much as you can. I work in an office setting, so I prepackage all of the items I am going to eat the night before. I usually put cooked oatmeal with dried cranberries, cinnamon, ground ginger, a bit of sugar, and a few almonds into a Pyrex container. Or, I put Greek yogurt, dried cranberries, almonds, and granola in a container. Those are my two "go-to breakfasts."

I always keep a can opener and cans of veggies that I like, and that are relatively low in calories, in my desk drawer. Two of my favorites are cut green beans and asparagus. In between meals, if I feel like I am starving, I open a can, put it in a cardboard cup, microwave it for 30 seconds, and eat the entire can of veggies.

Another snack that I like to keep in my bag is five or so wheat crackers. Sometimes I crave carbs, and five or so of those crackers will keep me going. Or, I purchase a small container of peanut butter and some Saltines from our cafeteria.

For lunch, I have several favorite meals that I pack and take with me. They include a Hummus sandwich on whole wheat bread, prepacked hummus and pretzel crackers, a bowl of homemade soup, or cottage cheese and crackers.

Afternoon snacks that I take with me to work include three or four dill pickles, a banana, an orange, and apple slices and peanut butter.

3. If you order your meals from a restaurant, plan ahead of time what you will order. I have several set meals I get from the truly wonderful café where I work. Often, I will get a to-go order of scrambled eggs and oatmeal. I will have the scrambled eggs for breakfast as a protein boost

and the oatmeal for lunch as nutritious "filler." I supplement these with the snacks I bring from home (canned veggies, fruit, crackers, peanut butter, etc.).

Another meal I like and that fits into my diet is the soup that the café serves — as long as it is not cream based.

I try to balance what I eat between the time I get up for work and when I come home from work — eating protein, grains, fruit, and veggies.

4. Hold something wonderful in reserve. I save a few things for my nighttime treats. These include two squares of chocolate, a small handful of chocolate covered raisins, or a small portion of some sweet that has lots of calories. I portion out just a small amount, and I know that that treat is there for me when I need it or at the end of the day.

5. Eat a "normal" dinner, just smaller portions with larger portions of veggies. My husband is a true "foodie." He actually pouts when I won't eat the meal that we had planned for dinner. I have tried serving him a "real" meal and eating a salad or another low-calorie meal, but he tells me that half of the fun of eating is sharing a meal, and then continues to goad me, asking, "Does it really make that big of a difference?" or "Are you really going to lose weight by not eating this nice meal with me?" or "It is no fun eating this pizza alone." I finally realized that if I even take a small portion of the "main" meal, and then supplement with veggies, he doesn't feel that I am having a different meal, and I get to have the satisfaction of trying the main course and supplementing with lower calorie/ healthy veggies so that I feel full.

6. Look for low calorie, filling treats that come in a variety of flavors. One of my favorite "treats" is a hot cup of tea. Have you visited the tea section of your grocery store lately? There are so many flavors! Even in small grocery stores, you can find over 20 types. And, there are many studies that show that tea is great for your health. Green

tea is loaded with antioxidants and may improve brain function, hasten fat loss, and lower the risk of cancer. And, green tea comes in amazing flavors. There also are many excellent black teas and herbal teas. My favorite black teas are Murchies teas from Canada. All named for things British, the teas are rich in multi-layered flavors. They are a bit expensive—but are a wonderful treat! My favorite herbal teas include ginger (nicely spicy), Rooibos, mint, and Red Zinger. Chamomile is nice for those nights when counting sheep doesn't make me fall asleep.

7. Okay, I admit it: I am addicted to coffee. I try to drink no more than 4-5 cups each day, but that is hard on some days. I can't drink it black; but with a splash of milk and a dash of sugar, it keeps me going throughout the day. And, at zero calories (the milk and sugar add just a few calories) it is a nice way to have several treats throughout the morning.

8. Water—contains zero calories and is filling. If you drink a glass of water before each meal, you will be well hydrated, will eat less, and will feel full faster.

9. Pickled anything! I try to keep several jars of pickles and pickled beets on hand for when I get a craving for something tart. I know that not everyone enjoys them, but they sure help me when I have a craving for a non-sweet treat.

10. Fresh grated Parmesan, green olives, and almonds—is a great combination! I know it is strange, but this is my mini-Italian snack when I want something salty. I mix together a couple of teaspoons of fresh grated Parmesan cheese, a few green olives, and about five almonds. It tastes very Mediterranean, and has a nice salty flavor.

11. Soups--Next to canned veggies to snack on and canned soups for a quick fix, homemade soups are my favorite diet food. I take four cans of broth, boil some chicken or fry ground turkey, add it to the broth with veggies and

seasonings, top with Parmesan cheese, and I have a wonderful meal!

12. Air-popped popcorn—this is my favorite movie or driving snack. I especially like the new versions that are seasoned, including black pepper popcorn.

13. Chocolate calcium chews and coconut oil chews--Vitamins and minerals can be tasty too. Every evening, I pop one or two chocolate calcium chews and a coconut oil chew.

14. Prunes -If you are like my husband, right now you are saying, "Yuck." But, I am a champion of prunes. First, they are like adult raisins, sweet with a tart undercurrent. Second, they are low in calories, yet relatively high in fiber. Last, they help keep your digestive tract "moving" which also is great when you are dieting, traveling, or prone to constipation. I keep a box in my fridge and chew on a couple as I exercise.

15. Chewing gum—I know that there are some diet experts who feel that chewing gum causes you to crave more food: you chew, and your stomach expects that food is on its way, and when it doesn't arrive, you become even hungrier. But, there are times, especially when I am doing desk work, that I find chewing gum to be satisfying, and I find that I don't have food cravings unless I truly am hungry. Some studies suggest that gum chewing can curb your appetite and improve your memory.

16. Planning ahead—I think it is important to have some "go to items" when you are craving something sweet, something sour, and something salty. The secret here is to think ahead to ensure that you have lower calorie items on hand that will address each of these types of cravings.

These are just a few of the foods and practices I use to support a healthy diet. One of the nicest components of Branch Living is that we share and learn from each other. I am looking forward to hearing your tips—I can always use more!

Physical Fitness

Okay, I'll admit it. I **hate** to exercise. My mom and dad are both habitual exercisers and have each asked me, "Don't you feel better after you have exercised?" My answer? "No." I dread exercising. I will find any excuse to not get on the treadmill or do any other form of exercise. And, if I procrastinate, it is just too late to exercise, right?

But, I do like what exercise does for me. I like the results. I like the fact that when I go to my doctor's office, my blood pressure is low. I am grateful that I exercise when I have to exert myself to shovel the walk, or push a loaded wheelbarrow around the yard, or chase after grandchildren. I don't get winded, and that is only because I **do** exercise.

I also like the fact that exercise helps me to keep my weight down. I try to burn at least 200 calories each session – that's more than 1,000 calories each week, and that helps a lot!

I sit a great deal in my job, and if I didn't exercise, I would not be able to consume many calories over the course of a day because I just don't burn that many – without making a conscious effort to push myself forward.

So, if I can exercise, as much as I dislike it, you can too.

I have just few tips to offer:

Develop some type of routine, and stick to it as much as possible. For example, I try to exercise every Friday, Saturday, and Sunday. My time on weekends is a bit more flexible, and I am more likely to find time to work in my 45-minute routine. If I am able to work in three exercise sessions during the weekend, then I only have to work in two more during the week to reach my goal of five sessions.

My routine consists of sit-ups, arm resistant exercises, and then 30 minutes on the treadmill on which I do a 200+ calories weight reduction routine that involves several "hills" (inclines).

75

On my "off" days, I still move. I stretch and use a mini-elliptical stepper for 10-minute increments.

I try to incorporate different exercises in my routine and during my off days just to keep it interesting.

Additionally:

I take the stairs whenever possible.

I hang out with friends who actually like to exercise. We go to an exercise class or do some outdoor activity (walking on trails, cross country skiing) and then reward ourselves afterward with a fun evening out.

I watch very little television, so when I work out on the treadmill, I "reward" (distract) myself with an interesting show and sometimes plan my time on the treadmill based on what half-hour program I want to see.

I also read magazines on the treadmill or listen to an audio book (anything to keep my mind off of the misery).

I know of several people who actually receive a cash reward for maintaining their health from their employer/insurance company. They use this is an incentive for exercising.

I have two dogs, and each one loves to go outside for a walk or a run. It is nice to spend a bit of time with them individually, and it gives me a great excuse to get outside and see what is going on in the neighborhood. We have many hills in our area, so walking a dog is a great workout.

How do you incorporate exercise into your life?

Share your ideas on Branchliving.org!

Reading

One of the "habits" that many people — myself included — strive to develop is setting aside time to read. Reading is pleasurable. Reading is informative. Given the right book, reading can be life changing. But, over 40% of Americans did not read a single book last year. So why don't we take time to read?

Like many things in life, reading gets pushed aside because it is not urgent and is not needed for daily living. We must prepare meals, wash clothes, help kids with homework, go to work, bathe, and grocery shop...but we have no urgent reason why we must read. Reading is quiet. A book just sits there and waits for you to decide to pick it up. You can put it down at any time. And, time passes, and you find that you have not picked up the book for days or even weeks. Yet, reading can provide you with insights to help you create a better life, be a better person, develop new skills, and reinforce new habits. Books can make you laugh, cry, think deeply, or just relax.

So, given the pressures in our crowded schedules to do the "urgent" or "necessary" and not the important or fulfilling, how do we make time to read?

Here are a few of the ways to work reading into a busy schedule:

1. Take reading with you. I frequently find myself with small snatches of down time. Such times occur when I am waiting for someone, for an event to begin, or for water to boil or the oven to preheat. I keep books close at hand — in my purse or carry bag, on my kitchen counter — so that when a few minutes open up, I can enjoy a page or two of my book.

2. Keep books in several places. I have books at my bedside, in my kitchen, in my car, in places where I am likely to sit down for a few minutes and relax. I keep books that I read on a regular basis at my bedside, but I also keep short reads, like devotionals, collections of short stories, and recipe books at locations where I might just find a few free minutes.

3. Collect books on a wide variety of interesting topics. When I have fiction, biographies, religious books, devotionals, or cookbooks to choose from, I can always find something that meets my current interests or mood.

4. Read book reviews or talk to friends to get recommendations on good books to read. Find people who like to read what you like to read, and find out what they are reading or have read. There are good websites for this as well.

5. Join a book club or a reading group. There is nothing like a deadline to push you forward in your reading. When you know that there is a date when you will be expected to have finished a book, you will be motivated.

6. Schedule time for reading. I don't have this opportunity as often as I would like, but I look forward to those snatches of quiet time whenever I can work them in.

7. Make reading a routine habit. I keep a book or two on my bedside table and make reading part of my nightly routine. I usually try to sneak in at least 10 minutes of reading before I turn out the lights.

8. Match reading to your style. Some people prefer electronic books, and others like to have a "real" book to hold in their hands. I find that I prefer traditional hardback or paperback books, but I like the convenience of electronic books when I am on the go. I also love to listen to audio books when I am cleaning, cooking, or driving.

How do you make time to read?

Share your ideas on Branchliving.org!

Finances

Okay, I hate to even touch this topic, because there are so many great experts on finances who offer sage advice. My favorite of these is Dave Ramsey. He is funny, smart, experienced, direct, and spirit-filled. So, my first piece of advice is to get yourself to a Financial Peace University course or buy the book. I have seen and heard of so many lives that have been turned around by following his wise counsel.

What I offer below are tips I have used to stash away extra cash and to save money over the past 30 years.

1. Take money out of your check before you get your check—this is my favorite way of saving money. First, I take my savings out of my check so that I never see it. I do this for my retirement savings. I did this for the funds I put aside for my three kids' college accounts. I do this for my Flexible benefit account, and I do this for some of my charitable giving. I don't allow myself to ever see the money, and so I don't miss it.

2. Fool yourself—I get 26 checks each year, one every two weeks. But, I live off of 24 checks. When those wonderful three-check months hit, I stash away the extra check. One of these pays for gifts throughout the year. The other goes to vacations, special items for the house, or needed repairs.

3. Follow the 10-10-80 rule (and then move down from the 80 as much as you can) – it is an old rule, but it works, which is why it has been handed down from generation to generation. Teach it to your children early in their lives. Save 10 percent of everything you earn. Give 10 percent of everything you earn to your church/ charities. Use the other 80 percent to live on. As you get funds in place, such as your emergency fund, start to try to give more and save more, and live on less.

4. I recently read that the typical Italian views life differently than the typical American. Americans often judge how wealthy someone is by how much they earn or by how much they spend. Italians judge wealth by how much you keep of what you earn. I

found this insightful and have never forgotten it. It doesn't matter how much you earn if you spend it all.

5. As I mentioned previously, Tim Keller's thoughts on Christians and wealth has always stuck with me. He says that Christians are needed in every income bracket so that we can have influence at every level. But, he cautions, Christians should live at the bottom of their income bracket so that they have plenty of resources to give to those in need and to the church. Living large is living foolishly.

6. Money is a tool. In your final days of life, you find that family, friends, faith hold the real value. Save for your retirement, and for those rainy days that will definitely come, but remember that your security and joy rest in God.

How do you use money well?

Share your ideas on Branchliving.org!

Organization

I am not an organized person by nature. But, I am blessed to be surrounded by people who are.

I have found that one of the best ways to become organized is to create space so that everything really does have its own space.

My husband, over time, has developed a passion to purge the house of things we don't need and don't use. I find it hard to get rid of anything because there is this little voice that says, "You may need that one day." And, occasionally that does happen. But, I also have found that those things I stash away for a rainy day are difficult to find when that rainy day arrives. I do such a good job of "stashing" that I don't have a clue where something is when I need it.

The Christian radio station I listen to each morning reported on a blogger who decided to get rid of 40 bags of items during the 40 days of Lent. The beauty of this was that she could bless others by giving items away that she wouldn't miss, and this would give her a spiritual detachment from things.

Once you have created the space, it is time to give everything a place. More than likely, you will discover at this point is that you still have too much stuff! Time to get rid of more!

When you have finally winnowed everything down to what you need and love, then it is time to get organized. I find organizing to be such an overwhelming project at times, that I break it into simple chunks of work—organizing a closet or even just a drawer—as opposed to an entire room. Once an area is organized, I try to hold the line. It is so tempting to chuck things away when you are in a hurry, but I have taught myself to let things sit out in piles where they will naturally bother me, rather than shoving them into a closet or drawer where they will stay until I have the energy to declutter once again. So start small, do it right, and plant your flag—THIS TERRITORY IS ORGANIZED—and then, take a breather before you take on the next project.

In terms of where to start, I find it best to list the top three messy areas that would make the biggest difference to me were they organized. I start with the smallest project and build up from there. I had a particular junk drawer in my kitchen that made me crazy. Every time I opened it, recipes, appliance manuals, coupons—you name it—fell out of the drawer as I dug into the mess looking for something. Once I found what I was looking for—or failed to—I would pat everything down and push hard on the drawer to shut it and conceal the disaster inside. One day, I had had it. I took everything out of the drawer and found out that more than half of what I had stored in it were things that had expired or that I would have never used. I used the 5S technique I learned in LEAN training (first used by Toyota in the 1970s). The 5S technique involves:

1. Sorting—separating needed items from those that are unneeded and eliminating that latter.

2. Straightening—assigning items to places where they will be easy to find.

3. Shining—keeping (the drawer) neat and clean

4. Standardizing—making it a habit to keep the drawer organized. No more putting clutter back in it!

5. Sustaining—developing a process to keep the drawer clean. In this case, I decided to put the recipes I cut out of magazines into a Tupperware container and the coupons into a small wicker chest.

The drawer organized, it was on to the closet. Success becomes rich soil for the next project.

If you are not naturally organized, it might be time to bring in a good friend who has this skill or a professional—yes, there are professionals who specialize in organizing for those of us who are less skilled.

If you don't have a friend or professional to lean on, you can research organizing tips on the Internet. I have gotten many good ideas through online sites and catalogs that offer organizing tools. Through a catalog, I learned of plastic wreath boxes to keep wreaths looking fresh from one year to the next.

My daughter is a natural organizer, proving once again that children don't get genes exclusively from their mothers! She uses boxes, Ziploc bags, and a black magic marker as her main tools. Everything that is not a display item is placed behind closed doors. I know that this isn't possible in every home—mine included. But to label items, to cluster them in ways that make sense, in places where it makes sense to store them (e. g. all of the office supplies together on one shelf), is a wonderful, simple way to begin!

Ditto books. Group them on shelves by topic, genre, author—it doesn't matter, just pick a system and use it! One of the nicest things my husband has done for me is to put all of my cookbooks together in one place. I used to waste so much time searching for a cookbook! Truly, that is the price of being disorganized—wasting time and money. Time spent hunting for an item that you cannot find, time shopping for a replacement if you don't find it, and the cost of replacing the item. Not to mention the frustration.

My final tip in this section is to try to make the project fun! Involve your spouse, child, or friend. Often, others can see order where I cannot. If you need to tackle the project alone, play fun music or listen to a good audio book. Plan a small treat for yourself in the end, though the organized spot is often reward enough!

How do you stay organized?

Share your ideas on Branchliving.org!

Volunteering

How many times have you said to yourself or to those around you, "I wish I had time to volunteer?" Volunteering seems to be part of how human beings are wired. Just as we are programmed to give of our material resources, we are designed to be good givers of our time as well.

According to the US Department of Labor, just shy of 25% of Americans reported volunteering in some way during the year. Volunteers on average give 52 hours of time per year. I suspect that the nearly 75% who did not donate time often wished they could find the time to donate!

Most volunteers were involved in one or two organizations. The organizations to which they contributed time included religious organizations (33.1% of volunteers), educational or youth services (25.2 %) and social or community service organizations (14.6 %).

And, what did these volunteers do? The top three activities were:

1. Collecting, preparing, distributing, or serving food (11.3%)

2. Fundraising (9.0%)

3. Tutoring or teaching (9.2%)

Not surprising, men were more likely to engage in general labor (12.3%) or coach, referee, or supervise sports teams (9.3%). Women were more likely to engage in the activities in the list above. Over 41.2% of those who volunteered did so because someone asked them to.

If you haven't been asked, don't wait for the invitation. Review in your mind nonprofits you support (in addition to your church): your library, humane society, homeless shelter, day care—think of the organizations you support that need your time—and give it!

Here are some steps to get started:

1. Make a list of the types of organizations you would like to support with your time, talents and money. Do a Google search or call your local chamber of commerce to find out which organizations in your community specifically address the areas you wish to support.

2. Research each as best as you can through the Internet, word of mouth, or friends who work at/ support/ know of the organization.

3. Pick your top three prospects.

4. Develop a list of questions the answers to which are important to you, such as:

a. How much/ little time do you need/ require of volunteers?

b. Does this time have to be scheduled or can you drop in to volunteer?

c. If the time needs to be scheduled, how far in advance do you need to sign up for time slots?

d. What skills do you seek?

e. Is there an orientation process?

f. Is there a trial period for serving?

g. Is the work primarily alone or in a group?

5. Go onsite and interview the person in charge of volunteers for the organizations you list as your top picks.

6. Make your commitment small and grow it if you'd like. Don't overcommit right off the bat. Volunteer jobs have a tendency to grow — so start small and be very realistic about how much of your time/ talent/ finances you can reasonably commit.

This habit directly supports the Almsgiving component of Branch Living. It is important for each of us — no matter how busy we are or feel — to be good givers of the resources we have.

Remember:

Each of you should give what you have decided in your heart to give, not reluctantly or under compulsion, for God loves a cheerful giver.
2 Corinthians 9:7

In what ways do you give of your time?

Share your ideas on Branchliving.org!

Learning Something New

You *can* teach an old dog new tricks. It just takes that dog a bit longer to get up to speed!

All through life, to stay relevant and stay in touch, we find that we need to pick up new skill sets. Those of us still in the workforce who are over the age of 50 have had to make a quantum leap in adjusting our skills to new technology that keeps changing faster and faster.

When I was in college, studying business, computers were just on the scene—and I mean "just." I remember going to the Information Technology Center to use a device to punch cards with little holes that, when stacked in place and fed into the computer, would tell the computer what to do. This computer was humongous. Each card had to be perfectly punched and in the right order, or the computer pitched a fit and spit all of the cards out. To incentivize us to use this beast, our instructors had developed clever programs that provided the student with a small reward if you got all of your punches just right and cards in the right order: the computer would spit out a "picture" of Snoopy or Batman or some cartoon character that was supposed to make us realize just how much fun this was!

Fast forward to today, when much of what we do in terms of "IT" can be done on our phones or tablets. Those of us in our mid-to-late career cycle have had to progress, painfully, through each new technology to get us to this point. But, I'll take a tablet or a smartphone over those cards any day. The point here is that technology advances at such a fast clip, we have to work constantly to stay ahead.

At home we've also seen many changes. We've gone from watching movies on television, to VHS tapes, then on DVDs, and now online. We've evolved from writing letters, to using email and now text each other to stay in contact. Each of these requires an understanding of a new technology.

These are the types of technological changes that we have to adjust to in order to stay connected to our world. But, there is a different type of learning that is equally important. It is the type of learning that helps us grow in our quest to fulfill our purpose and contribute to Christ's Kingdom.

For example, you might volunteer at a homeless shelter and find that you have a gift for counseling that you would like to take further. To move this goal ahead, you may need to take coursework in counseling. Do it!

Or, you may be confused as to what you would like to do to with your life. There are classes you can take to help you discover your gifts and talents. Take them! Do the work!

Or, you might have always wanted to play the piano, learn a new language, or learn how to cook special meals. Try it. Make time to develop the special skills that match your passions!

The point here is that often it is scary as we get older to take on new and difficult challenges. We get into a rut, but somehow, that rut becomes terribly easy to remain in, and so when we hear that nagging voice telling us to try something new, we are too frightened and too comfortable to change.

Here are some tips on how to get out of your rut and start learning:

1. Search your local community college's adult learning offerings. This is a wonderful way to explore a new hobby or even a potential career change. There are a wide variety of classes to choose from: photography, web design, genealogy, fitness, cooking—you name it. Community colleges often offer a single "exposure" class to whet your appetite to see if you enjoy the subject before investing much time or money. If you like the class, you can sign up for a more in depth semester course. Who knows? A whole new career could follow!

2. Take an online course. There are thousands of opportunities to take courses at your own pace. Search sites that often offer promotional deals for Internet courses on such topics as Writing Children's Literature, Project Management, or Introduction to Writing Computer Applications.

3. See what your local stores offer. A supermarket near my parents' house offers cooking classes. A yarn shop near where we used to live offered knitting classes one night each week. These local offerings are a great way to test the waters and to make new friends.

4. Start a learning group of your own. I lived in a very small town for a number of years, and the nearest community college was 45 miles away. I didn't have time during the week to make the drive to take classes, so I asked a number of my talented friends to have a ladies night out once each month, during which one of the women would teach a new art, craft, or cooking technique or would invite an "instructor" to teach the group new skills. Because the women had differing interests, we learned a variety of skills, and we had fun while we did it. Start a group of your own! Invite friends who have varying interests. If you don't know whom to invite, put a notice in your church newsletter or let your local community organizations or clubs know of your interest in starting a group. If you don't want to host the new group in your home, ask your minister if you could use a room in the church. Ask a local coffee shop or restaurant owner if you could use a room or a section of the establishment once each week.

5. Find a mentor. There are many experts in a wide array of fields right where you live. I have found that most people are flattered when asked if someone may shadow them for a few hours. If you have the desire to arrange flowers, call a florist several miles away (so that you might not eventually compete with that person), and ask if you could job shadow and be an extra set of hands for that

individual. If you want to write a column, invite a columnist to lunch (pay for that lunch!) and discuss how to break into the profession, how to develop your writing skills, how to move ahead.

Don't sit with your dreams; make them happen! How are you doing that today?

Share your ideas on Branchliving.org!

Healthy Sleep

In a study completed in 2014, 45% of Americans stated that poor or insufficient sleep affected their daily activities at least once during the past week. At least one-third of Americans are sleep deprived. Why is this?

Unlike times in the not so distant past, the world today, it seems, never goes to sleep. I remember when I was a girl, staying up until 11 p.m. or so on weekends, watching one of the four available channels until the bitter end. I knew it was time to go to bed when the station played the Star Spangled Banner along with a film of the American flag blowing in the wind, and that was the end of the broadcast day. From then until six o'clock the next morning there was only a still image that looked like a black and white dartboard (smaller circles inside of larger circles). But, the television station went off the air, and it was time for the world to go to sleep.

This was my experience, but if you could go back much further, before there were electric lights, bedtime came much earlier. Sometime try turning off all of the lights and reading by candlelight or firelight. Before long, you will decide to go to bed and wait for daylight.

Today, there is never a compelling reason to go to bed other than fatigue. Many of us — myself included — often don't feel the fatigue of a late night until the next morning, when obligations prevent us from making up the sleep we have missed. And so the cycle repeats itself. There is always more to do, and artificial light permits us to get it done.

But here are the facts: According to WebMD, sleep deprivation can lead to 10 significant health problems. These are: greater risk of accidents, reduced ability to think clearly, greater risk of serious health concerns (heart attacks, stroke, diabetes), less interest in sex, increase in depression or anxiety, aging of the skin, more forgetfulness, increased likelihood of weight gain, impaired judgment, and increased risk of death. So clearly, we all need to get an adequate amount of sleep!

Here are a few tips that have helped me in my quest to get more and better sleep:

1. Planning my evening backwards: When I come home from work, I try to set up my night to go to bed in time to have 7-8 hours of sleep. I first calculate the time I need to get up and then work backwards. For example, if I have to get up at 6 a.m., I know that I have to be in bed between 10 and 11 pm. I tend to stall at the end because I hate to go to bed before midnight. So, I pick 10:30 p.m. as the target, knowing that I will probably not make it to bed until 11. I look at the time I made it home from work, let's say 6 p.m., so I have 5 hours left. I know it will take me a full half hour to putz around, get changed, decompress, and get on with my evening. Deduct 45 minutes for dinner. I am now down to 3 hours and 45 minutes. Deduct 45 minutes for exercise (5 nights a week), and 30 minutes for Bible study and 15 minutes for devotions. Now I am down to 2 hours and 15 minutes, and I will while away at least 15 minutes by now, so at best I have 2 hours. I spend 30 minutes online catching up on emails/ blogs/ news stories. I spend a half hour catching up with my husband or kids and then I try to spend at least 30 minutes on my latest project and

then 30 minutes for showering and getting ready for the next day.

Now, items get moved in and out of this idealized schedule. Once each week, I have our Life Group if I can make it. And, I usually have at least two evening meetings every week.

But, this idealized schedule shows you why I no longer have much time for television.

To stay on track with my Branch Living, I have to structure my evenings to create room in my schedule to achieve my goals. And, television gets put on the back burner.

When I had children at home, this type of schedule was even more challenging. And, it was even more difficult when I was working, raising children, and getting my Master's degree at night. Much more difficult.

2. Don't expect perfection when your schedule implodes (which it regularly does) — I know from experience that there are times when my idealized schedule cannot happen. I then have to decide which items get moved off of the schedule. If I have exercised for three days, I move that day's session off schedule. I try to hold to the bedtime to have seven hours of sleep (at least).

3. Don't worry if you can't fall asleep — even rest is a good thing. Try to relax and go in your mind to a place that you find peaceful. Relax your mind, and as images of troubles or problems come to mind, remind yourself that you will have all day tomorrow to think about these things.

4. If you feel you need to sleep and you can't, ask your physician if you can take Melatonin. I would not take it without a physician's advice, and I would only take it as needed, but it is a natural product in the vitamin aisle. I take it on those nights when I go to bed with my brain still

racing from the day's events, and I know sleep is still quite a distance off.

5. Turn off all electronic devices an hour before you need to sleep, and let your mind completely relax. I find this step particularly difficult, but I force myself to have quiet time by scheduling non-electronic events before bed, e.g. Bible study and showering.

These are just a few of the techniques I have used to try to increase the amount of quality sleep I get each night. You will devise your own.

My final advice on this subject: Pray each night before you try to drift off to sleep, giving all of your concerns and troubled thoughts over to God. Let Him carry the burden of the items left at the end of your day. He'll manage just fine!

How is your sleep quality? What is your regular sleeping pattern?

Share your thoughts, ideas, and concerns on Branchliving.org!

Travel

Although travel is not a "habit" for most of us, it is one of those experiences that we often wish we could do more often, but time and/ or money often serve as barriers.

In nearly every case when I have taken the time and spent the money to travel, I have been so grateful for the experience and have relived the memories over and over. So, I have learned to create room for travel in my calendar and in my budget. I will never see all of the places I desire to see, but I will give it my best shot to see as many as I can and stay within our budget.

Travel gives you time to think about your life. It opens your mind to new thoughts, new ways of doing things. In my case, I am on the phone, in meetings or emailing much of my day, so I find travel to be a time when I can downshift my mind a bit. Usually, it takes a full day for me to realize that I am not on a schedule, that I can relax. I take a full day to transition, usually while I am on the plane, train or travelling in the car. I try to take only a few work materials with me, though I do confess that I check my emails to ensure that all is well back home.

In addition to giving my mind a chance to downshift, I find that travel does something else wonderful for my brain. It allows my mind the space it needs to think new thoughts, dream, and imagine. The new setting provides new experiences, and those new experiences often lead to new ways of thinking, new ideas, and new plans.

Travel also provides my husband and me — or my entire family — the opportunity to reconnect. We talk more, listen more, and grow closer in our relationship. Time away from responsibilities allows essentially uninterrupted time to focus on each other and on the setting that we are in.

Although it is often difficult to make friends in new places, you can make new acquaintances. On train rides, bus trips, group trips, cruises, there is plenty of time to chat with other travelers. We also have had interesting conversations with other travelers at bed and breakfast establishments we have stayed at. When you are sitting at the breakfast table with people, you naturally talk about where you are from, what you plan to do that day, what you have already seen, and conversation just flows naturally.

Travel broadens your horizon, deepens you appreciation of our wonderful world, and creates time and space for new ideas!

You don't have to go far to "travel." You just need to get out of your current environment. Go camping. Stay at a lodge. Rent a cabin. Just get away — from phones, work, and all distractions, and enjoy your new surroundings!

Here are ways we find time and money to travel:

1. Plan ahead — we have found that often, if we plan months out, we can secure good prices on all types of reservations. And, we don't risk finding that there are no seats/ rooms available. For example, the lodges and cabins in national parks fill quickly for summer months.

2. Look for last minute deals — although this is opposite of the tip above, it is also a good and notable way to save money. If your schedule is flexible, and if you can take off at the last minute, often airlines and hotels have excess capacity that they hope to fill. They hold off for so long, and then often slash the prices as they get closer to the dates they need to fill.

3. Get points on credit cards, dining cards, hotel stays, etc. for future travel — I only advise this if you truly pay off your credit cards every single month, on time, without fail. If you don't do this, the money you are paying in interest can easily outweigh any points you are earning. But, if you are diligent about paying off your credit cards every single month, you can rack up points for travel to nice places!

4. Look at renting a house or an apartment through online sites — my only caveat here is to be very careful when doing this. I personally know of friends who have traveled to a destination, only to find that the place they rented does not exist, and their deposit was never recovered through this scam. But, I also have friends who regularly travel this way, securing private taxi services and rooms through sites on a routine basis, and they have had good experiences. Just keep in mind that there is a downside to all of these privately arranged sites — some travelers have been physically endangered through unsavory predators. This is certainly not the norm, but please be careful!

5. A somewhat safer way of making private travel arrangements is through a group, club or association to which you belong. For example, I belong to a ladies group that has chapters throughout the United States. Some of

the women in different chapters "rent" out rooms in their homes for brief stays, and the money goes to benefit the group. The women have to register the availability of their rooms on the nationwide website and you have to be an enrolled member to access to the list. This is a more "controlled" situation than booking a private residence, sight unseen, online.

6. Consider renting places where you can cook — eating out on the road is expensive. Try to rent rooms/ houses/ cabins that have a refrigerator, microwave, toaster oven and coffee pot. Just these few appliances are all you need to keep from having to spend a lot of money at expensive restaurants. If you do eat out, you can take part of your restaurant meal back to your room for a later snack.

7. If you do want to eat out, do it at lunchtime and cook dinner. Lunch is often half the price of dinner. When we travel with our children, we ask each couple to take a turn making dinner. In this way, no one gets stuck in the kitchen all the time.

8. Visit the local bakeries, cheese shops, meat shops, produce stands, and pack a picnic for the road. It is cheaper, healthier, and you will meet some nice shop owners and eat local food!

9. Make sure your auto insurance will cover your rental car — this is so important. Often, even though it is more expensive, it is worth the money to take out insurance on the rental car itself. I had read this in a magazine one time, and the next time my husband and I travelled to Arizona, we took out insurance on the rental car. About three days into our trip, we were at a stoplight. I glanced out my side mirror and saw a Mercedes Benz barreling at us, with no signs of stopping. There was a sudden "crash" and our car was jolted forward. Thankfully, the light had changed just as we felt the impact, and the car in front of us had already

started forward, so we weren't sandwiched between two cars.

10. Pack travel items — airports will gouge you for items such as aspirin, batteries, even gum. Go to a store prior to flying or taking the train. Stock up on any convenience items, snacks, or over the counter medications you might need.

You also can combine your "alms" with travel by going on a church-sponsored mission trip, in an area that has long-standing ties to such sponsored groups (not those where groups come and go without a coordinated on-the-ground presence). Many benefits can come out of such trips including making new friends, learning new skills, or developing an appreciation for how others live and a better understanding of the many blessings you have in your everyday life back home.

My son's life took a whole new direction based on a mission trip he completed while in high school. He and several of his friends went on a school-sponsored trip to an inner city church where they helped paint rooms and lead a youth worship session. This was during his junior year in high school. The next year, when he was a senior, he was deciding what college to go to and he felt attracted to a college he had visited while on the mission trip. He attended that college, and there, he met his future wife. God can use our willingness to leave our comfort zone and step out to bless us and others in amazing ways.

Travel is eye opening, relaxing, and can be life changing.

Please share your stories and tips with us! There are always new ways to save money, stay safe and secure, and see the world. Share your ideas at Branchliving.org!

Chapter 8

Putting It All Together

If you are like most of us, at this point, you have a wonderful list of goals. And you are revved up to make the commitment to achieve these goals! Good work! You are almost there!

You now need a hefty dose of reality. You need to look at your resources. Specifically, you need to look at the time you can commit and the money you have to spend (if your goals require financial resources) so that you have a realistic plan that does not overwhelm you. It is far better to accomplish 3-5 goals – and then go to your bank of goals for more successes, than it is to plan out 15 goals, get discouraged, and accomplish none of them. I speak from experience! This happens far too often! So, before we develop your Branch Living plan, we are going to plot it out for success.

Take each of your goals. One by one, list the resources you will need to accomplish the each. List the total amount of time you estimate it will take to accomplish the goal. The time in total, the time each month, the time each week. You should estimate high— if you think it will take an hour per week, estimate two hours per week. It is better to have more time than less. Give yourself room in your schedule for "off" weeks. There will be weeks when you aren't feeling well, when "life happens" and you just don't have time to focus on your goals. Build in a bit of a fudge factor to enhance your chances for success.

Here is an example of how to "break" down a goal.

Let's say you want to find a church family within the next three months. Your first task is to break this goal down into its subparts.

1. Review websites for information on local churches.
2. Talk to Christian friends whom you know and admire and ask where they go to church and what they do/ don't like about their churches.
3. Visit three-to-five churches.
4. Review their statements of belief to ensure that they hold the Bible as their standard – we need that anchor on which to build our lives.
5. Attend events at those churches you like; ask to sit in on a small group (if available).
6. Narrow your selection.
7. Attend the church that is number 1 on your list for three months.
8. If satisfied, join the church – if not, go back to other churches on list and repeat the process.

Take each of your goals, break each down into measurable, defined, smaller categories and put each within a time frame.

This next step is crucial: how many hours each week would you need to achieve the narrowed list of goals you have selected?

To illustrate this: let's say you have the following broad goals:

Bond

Study two pages of my Bible, five times each week, with my commentary.

Relationships

Enroll in two social programs — one at church and one in my community — to meet new people.

Work to heal the relationship with my neighbor.

Alms

Volunteer twice each month at the local animal shelter.

New/ Renew

Lose 15 pounds this year.

Exercise for 30 minutes, five times each week.

Church

Attend the new Bible study each week.

Join a small group.

Habits

(In addition to those needed to meet the above goals – in other words, all others).

Read a 15-minute Devotion once each week.

Whew!

Now, you need to determine — realistically — how much time you have in your day and week to devote to your goals. This sounds easy, but it is truly a period of soul searching.

You need to take a realistic look at your schedule. Let's take my goal list as an example. As I previously mentioned, I work outside of the home. I usually get home between 6 p.m. and 7 p.m. and I have to be in bed by 11 each night. When I take out time to talk with my husband, eat dinner, get ready for the next day, I have about 1-½ hours to 2 ½ hours to devote to my goals on weekdays.

This is where it is painful: you take ½ of the time you know you have. This is "realty." So, in my case, on weeknights (work nights), realistically, I have an hour and a half to devote to my goals. For those that need to occur on a regular basis, (in my case, Bible study, devotions, and exercise), I need to spread these on my calendar so that I can "make room" and devote myself to them. This has involved lifestyle changes and has meant that much of what I do to meet my goals must occur on weekends.

My best advice is to give yourself plenty of time to achieve your goals. And, take a very hard look at how you spend your discretionary time so that you can make very good use of it.

In my case, as I stated earlier, I needed to eliminate all television watching — with the exception of two weekly shows — during the week. It was the only way I could meet my goals and look back on my year well pleased with how I had spent my time — my life — that year. It took time and discipline, but it worked!

So, to meet my goals, I use my discretionary time during the week to: exercise, read my Bible and devotions, attend my Life Group twice each month, and work on my writing.

Everything else on my goal list gets moved to the weekend, and that means I cannot just "chill" on my weekends, as I would prefer to do! I make room on my weekends for my relationship goals, my giving opportunities, my volunteer work, my church activities (except for my Life group), and my other goal areas. My weekend also is "catch up" time for areas where I have fallen behind.

I have learned the hard way that the attainment of my goals — in fulfillment of Branch Living — requires that I make changes in the way I structure my time, that I take a realistic view of how much time it truly takes to get things done, and that I make sacrifices to live the life I REALLY want to live.

So, set your goals and pattern out your "average" week. See if you realistically have enough time to achieve your goals. If you don't, pare down the number of goals you set for yourself. Try to keep one in each of the main categories: Bond, Relationships, Alms, New/ Renew, and Church. If there are habits you want to make or break that don't neatly fit into one of these categories, pick the one you most want to achieve. This will give you 5-6 goals. Now, see if your week can accommodate the amount of time these goals will require.

Once you have defined the time needed to achieve your goals, you will need to see if you have the other resources you need in order to move forward. Do your goals involve money, such as taking lessons, signing up for classes, or hiring a personal trainer? Do you have funds set aside to meet these goals? If not, how will you go about earning the money you need?

Don't set yourself up for failure! Ensure that you have the needed resources to meet your goals.

Now, it is time to begin setting up your year, then your month, then your week to reach your goals. Work backwards, so that when you are done with this year, you will have achieved what you set out to do by the steady pace you make each week and each month. Set aside time when you can catch up on goals or make greater progress. For example, there are times when I can't visit my kids. I set aside time to Skype with them or time to write a nice long email so that we stay in touch. There are times when I can't attend my Life Group as often as I would like, so I try to keep up with the group by watching the online video streamed messages that they are discussing. Find alternate ways to achieve the same goal. If you can't volunteer this month at the local library, bake a quick batch of cookies for the staff. Find ways you can meet your goals, but in a different way, when you hit the wall and you can't make your original goal work.

Once you have worked backward, planning what you need to achieve in a year, each month, each week to achieve your goals for this year, it is time to start plotting out your first month of your "new year" ("new" is whenever you choose to start!).

I use a calendar that that is in a journal format. I do keep an electronic calendar in my computer and in my phone as well, but for my personal goals, I much prefer a calendar that I write on. Why? Because I like to hold my goal calendar in my hands. I like to write down my successes and journal about my less successful progress toward my goals. I think when you write, track, and journal, your goals seem even more "real."

The first pages of my journal/ planner follow the steps of Branch Living for each area (B-R-A-N-C-H) – Dream, Delve, Discover, Decide, Do It!. I next have a page, "Putting It All Together," that helps me to whittle my goals to a manageable level, charting the time and resources/ finances each will take. Once I have pared down my goals and have my final listing, I place them on the next page, "Plot Out Your Goals." Here I estimate the time it will take to complete each goal for the year, each month, and each week. Once I see that I have a manageable/ affordable list of goals, I complete a refined listing of my goals.

Next, I take my "Plot Out Your Goals" page and plot out what I need to achieve each month—or determine which month(s) I will work on specific components of a goal. I use this as my cheat sheet to outline my plan on a sheet entitled "The Plan." This is done just once each year—and modified only when you want to modify your annual goals. Here, I write all my goals under the headings "Bond," "Relationships," "Alms," "New," "Church," and "Habits." "The Plan" is a graph that I complete – with my goals down the left side of the page and the months of the year across the top. Into each square, I plot out the goal achievement I need to realize and the month I need to realize it in. Some goals I work on each month, and in these cases, I put an amount in each month (e.g. how many pounds I would like to lose or the weight I hope to reach month by month; the number of pages of my devotional I hope to read, etc.). In other cases, I put an "X" in the month where I plan to achieve a goal. For example, if I plan to outline my book in the month of March, I simply put an "X" under March. In the very last column, I put my goal amount for the entire year, so I can monitor my progress toward my annual goal. I complete "The Plan" at the beginning of the year, and then I duplicate the form on a second form entitled "My Achievements," listing the goals down the left hand side and the months across the top – but I leave all of the squares on the graph blank. Here, I will chart my progress toward my goals, each month, at the end of the month.

I then turn to the first month in my calendar. I have a page at the beginning of the month entitled "Monthly Goals." Here, I fill in the goals for the month that I listed on "The Plan" graph. I duplicate that list on a Tally Sheet, right behind the goal sheet, where I can chart my weekly progress.

Next, my calendar has a "week at a glance" that encompasses two pages. Each Saturday night, I look over my month of goals to see if I can still place my specific goals from my "month at a glance" into my week as I had planned. I make adjustments as needed and then enter the daily goals enter into my calendar as my schedule permits. Then, during the week, I "work my plan." When a day takes a turn that I had not anticipated, I readjust my schedule and move on. As long as I make consistent, steady progress, I stay motivated and satisfied that I am "Branch Living" in between Sunday worship.

I have a "Keeping Track" form in my calendar in the middle of each week. This is my favorite form — by far — because here I credit myself with progress every day. My calendar is set up with a "leaf" for each of the seven days of the week. I fill in the leaf if I meet my daily goal. Goals that are set for once each week are listed at the bottom with a leaf in front of each. If I achieve that goal, I am done with it for the week."

At the end of each week, put your achievements on your monthly tally sheet under the column designated for that week. Complete the new weekly calendar and the new "Keeping Track" form for the upcoming week. At the end of the month, use your monthly Tally sheet to record your monthly accomplishments on your annual "My Achievements" form at the front of your journal. Reassess where you are in your goal achievements through reflection and review of your accomplishments. I know this seems very complicated. As I read over how to track achievements in this section, I thought "How will anyone follow this?" For that reason, I have developed a journal that perfectly matches the outline in this section. You can purchase that journal for ease of use — or you can develop your own method. The key is to set goals, track accomplishments, and make adjustments.

In your end-of-the-month assessment, describe what stood in your way of meeting your goal, how you will regroup, set a new goal, and move forward. Don't give up! Pilots call this "course correction." When they need to get back on the flight path they make subtle corrections. You can do the same. Branch Living isn't about demonstrating perfection. It is about living our imperfect, flawed lives in the best way we can to stay on course, using our gifts, and living the lives we are designed to live.

Be flexible. If you have a period of time when you just can't move ahead with work on your goals, don't fret. Start fresh as soon as you can!

For example, I had two-month period when I was on the road a great deal, visiting family and attending meetings for work. I found it nearly impossible to find time to exercise. So, for two months straight, I fell behind on this goal, which also impacted my weight loss goal. When I was able to get back into a more "normal" rhythm, I put a stronger emphasis on these two goals, scheduling my time on the treadmill and shopping for veggies to take to work to help curb my appetite.

The important thing is not to allow yourself to get discouraged or give up on your goals just because you fall behind. If you need to, adjust your year-end goals and get back on track.

Trust me. You will feel better about yourself at the end of the year if you achieve a portion of your goals than you will if you quit and achieve none of them. Also, if you see yourself making progress at the year's end, it will give you a boost to start your new year of goals.

Never give up. Never quit. Pick yourself up. Revise your goals. Get back at it. You will feel so much better about yourself. I promise!

It is most important to end strong. A strong ending of a month or a year serves as a wonderful springboard for the next month or year. If you are dragging at the end, it is harder to jump-start your goals for the new year, but even then, it can be done if you let go of the past year and look at the fresh calendar ahead.

Chapter 9

Rewards

When it comes to rewards, I tend to go against much of the advice I have read. For example, I have read that if you are trying to lose weight, you should never make food a reward. I agree that if a substance you are trying to remove from your diet is harmful, you should not use it as a reward. However, if you are trying to lose weight, and a certain treat can motivate you toward your success, by all means, use it!

When I am dieting, I have certain treats I allow myself to have as rewards along the way, such as a certain chocolate bar that combines dark chocolate and black pepper. When I reach some of the "big" target goals, I enjoy a meal out with my husband at a restaurant that I don't go to until the goal is met.

It is not that I am "driven" by food, but in the case of dieting, I know that there are certain treats that help motivate me to make my goal. I keep a candy bar in my desk as a treat for a three pound loss. I see that candy bar each time I open my drawer, and I remember that I am dieting and that there is a reward if I can meet my next goal.

Setting rewards requires that you ask yourself several key questions:

1. What small items would serve as motivators for me?
2. (If the rewards involve money) How much money can I set aside to ensure that I will be able to have the item when I meet the goal?
3. How can I tie these small items to the achievements that I need to make?
4. What larger rewards can I put in place that will motivate me to move forward and help me meet my big milestone goals?

I try to tie my small rewards to the actual goal itself. For example, when I set devotion time or reading the Bible as a goal, I purchase a devotional or Bible Commentary before my goal-period has begun. I look for used books or shop online for gently used copies of books. If I can't find what I like in an affordable range, I ask for the book for Christmas -or ask for a bookstore gift card to help offset the cost. I have found that you can have a low budget and still find ways to afford nice, small motivators!

It is very important to not set your goals out of your price range. This will only cause stress in your life, and stress tends to distract us from our goals. Set a budget—even if it is just a few dollars—and stick to it! Be creative! Remember, not all rewards have to cost money! Here are just a few of my favorite rewards that do not cost much, if anything:

- A spa evening, in my own home—replete with nice body creams, a warm bubble bath, a pedicure, and nice music
- A day off of work, in which I control the agenda—sleeping in, reading a book outside with a cup of tea, watching the sunset, all things I often do not make time for

- A day of "thrifting" where I go to some of my favorite second-hand stores
- An afternoon spent at two or three bookstores
- A shoulder-rub from my husband
- A bar of organic chocolate
- A Skype/Facetime session with family
- A long walk with the dogs
- A movie night with my husband
- A bouquet of fresh flowers

Some of my moderately priced rewards include:

- A new article of clothing
- A new piece of jewelry
- A new accessory — such as a scarf
- A limited shopping spree on Etsy
- A meal at a restaurant
- A girls' night out

Some pricier items include:

- A vacation
- A weekend getaway
- A spa day (or a spa service)
- A new outfit

Use your imagination! Again, you do not need any pricey rewards! The joy is in meeting the goal—and the reward is just an outside reminder to you that you rock!

It is good to make an effort to tie the reward to the goal. Likewise, it is often good to start to use a reward as a "launch pad" for a goal.

For example, this year, I purchased three new small pieces of exercise equipment— all three for under $100—to incentivize me toward my exercise goal.

Other examples of launch pads for goals include:

- A new blender for a smoothie diet
- A share in a local farm's produce (CSA), for your new diet
- A jump rope for exercise
- A new Bible for your private time with God
- The enrollment fee to a new class — for the future you or to make friends — or both!
- A nice box of stationery to catch up with old friends
- Gift cards to fast food restaurants to hand out the next time you see someone in need
- Ditto gas cards
- A gift card to a local florist for flowers on your church altar
- A gift certificate for a dinner out for your minister and his wife

The list goes on and on — but these purchases jump start your goal achievement and are nice, visible signs that you are serious about moving ahead!

I know that some people "poo-poo" rewards — but they have always helped me move forward toward achieving my goals. If they work for you, go for it!

Here are a few tips:

- It helps to set up your rewards early on — perhaps as early as the "dream" part of your goal setting.
- Make sure that your rewards are affordable and achievable (within your ability to obtain).
- Before you settle on your rewards, decide what it is specifically that motivates you.
- Look for rewards that match your goals (e.g. a writing journal for your journaling goal).
- Set your reward levels at less than 100%. For example, "If I achieve 80% of this goal, I will reward myself with ____."
- You can involve others in your rewards (e.g. a back rub from you husband) but make sure that they are onboard.

If you REALLY want to tempt yourself, purchase your reward in advance, and have someone "hold" it for you — so that you won't get the reward until you achieve the goal. This is the supreme motivation because you have spent the money/ invested in the reward, but you can't enjoy it until you have achieved the goal or the benchmark. Wow — that is motivating!

Okay — it is your turn to get started! Look through the goals you have set. If you are motivated by rewards, tie a reward to each of your goals or to benchmarks you have set along the way to your goal achievement. Post photos of your rewards where you can see them so they will motivate you. Review your progress toward your benchmark rewards and toward the completion of your final, goal-completion reward. Remind yourself at least monthly of where you are in your progress toward each goal. Enter the rewards as a reminder on the "Notes and Rewards" section of the "Month at a Glance" calendar.

Rewards can often be that little "pick me up" that keeps you going.

Chapter 10

Pruning, Grafting, Charting

"Nothing can stop the man with the right mental attitude from achieving his goal; nothing on earth can help the man with the wrong mental attitude."
Thomas Jefferson

If you have set up your goals in a tracking system, you will be able to quickly determine if you have overreached, set your goals too low, or have a system that is "just right" (Goldilocks). This realization will come to you very early in the process.

If you have overreached, it is time to prune back your goals. Do this very early in the process because you will become discouraged if you don't stay on course and will be tempted to throw in the towel on the whole process. Trust me. I have been there.

For example, if you have set a goal of reading three pages of the Bible each day and find at the end of your week that you have read a scant five pages in total, readjust your goal. Cut back on the number of pages. Set the goal based on time — not on the number of pages. "I will read the Bible for 20 minutes each day." If you have bought one of the "Read the Bible in One Year" books, expand it to two years — even three years. The point is do not give up! This is not a race. Sometimes, you have to take smaller bites of the elephant to accomplish the bigger goal.

As an aside, especially in the area of "Bonding," you are not seeking a race to the top — you are seeking a relationship with God. Quality time with God, increasing the depth of your understanding of Him, deepening your understanding of what He means to you and what He is doing within you is what you are seeking — not a race through the pages of the Bible. So, if you need to slow down, do so. You have my permission. ☺ The goal isn't to finish the Bible in one year. The goal is to have a deeper relationship with God by the end of the year. This is one area you cannot afford to stop. Slow and steady growth in your relationship with God is the goal.

If you find that it is "way easy" for you to work your plan, and you have a great deal of extra time (lucky you!), then you might want to "graft in"/ add in some new goals. Go back to your original list. If there are some goals you didn't include in your initial plan, add one or two now. But, again, do not overwhelm yourself. Better to achieve three goals than to start with ten goals and achieve none.

The main point is to keep working your plan. Your plan should be a living document. You should add and subtract as needed to keep moving forward. Don't give up!

There have been very stressful times in my life when I have literally set my plans/ goals aside for six weeks to devote myself to a major issue at hand: the illness of a loved one, a major project at work, etc. I make a note in my journal that I took a needed respite, and then I plunge back in when the major issue has passed.

One cautionary note: when you are setting your goals or making your plans, you might want to incorporate "break" periods. For example, if you know that you are taking a week's vacation out of town in the summer, work that into your plan—scale back your goal expectations for that month, and then incorporate this reduced number into your annual goals. As the saying goes, "Life happens," and if you can anticipate when you will not be able to work on your goals, it is better to work that in during the early stages of your planning. If you didn't anticipate or incorporate these breaks in your schedule/ goals, make the modification as you go. As mentioned earlier, this is a midway course adjustment and nothing more.

I have learned that the two weeks before Christmas and the week following Christmas are just too full for me to make progress on many of my goals. And, so, when I draft my annual plan, I take that into account. I don't beat myself up because I can't do it all. I know I can't, and so I plan around those very busy times.

Another way to make these accommodations is to work ahead, so that when your break period comes, you are already ahead in your achievements. For example, if you are going to be on vacation for two weeks, and you plan to write a loved one every two weeks, write two letters before you leave. You'll still be on track when you return.

With these cautionary notes, it is time for you to begin to plot out your goals in terms of progress month by month. Here is an example of what I mean.

Let's say I plan to lose 20 pounds over the course of one year. That averages to about a pound and a half each month. So, I might look at the year ahead and plan out those months in which it might be easier to lose weight and plan to lose two pounds during those months—even three—and then cut back on the weight I plan to lose on months where it might be harder to meet this goal, such as vacation months or the Thanksgiving/ Christmas seasons. Or, I can plot my weight loss goal at a rate of a pound and a half each month, and then slow it down for the seasons when I don't anticipate losing as much weight. In this case, I cut my annual goal down from 20 pounds to say 15, anticipating that I will have periods of little weight loss.

Take time to reevaluate each or your goals in light of events that you know will take place. You also can do this in the middle of the year if unforeseen events creep up on you. Reevaluate, reset your goals, and move ahead. Better to stay on track and not get discouraged than to become overwhelmed and throw in the towel!

Okay—pick up your journal, reevaluate, and reset your goals for success!

Chapter 11

Trusting God

One of the hardest parts of the Christian walk for me — and this is not universally supported within the Christian faith — was to come to grip with the realization that nothing comes into my life without it first passing through God's hands. It was a hard truth for me to embrace initially, but now it is one that gives me great comfort and assurance when I am going through rough times.

Again, not all Christians embrace this belief, and it is not a "core" part of the Christian walk. The belief is based on viewing God as having control over everything and yet allowing us to have free will. The perspective is that when something bad comes into your life, God permitted it in your life, even though you are His beloved child, because it will make you stronger, better, more humble, more giving...who knows? When you treat the hard things that enter into your life as times to cling tighter to God, to your faith, and to grow, it is certainly easier to get through them.

Why is this belief included in goal setting? I add it here because you can plan for the very best year, have all of your ducks lined up, plan your work and work your plan and then suddenly, out of nowhere, tragedy strikes. So what do you do? Give up? Chuck the plan? Say to yourself, "I should have known this would never work!"

No. What you do is pause. Pause completely. You set aside your plan, and you take the time you need to reassess the situation. You do not move ahead until you have a full assessment of the situation, and you are able to know how to successfully move ahead. Only then should you take the next step.

I have had several times in my life like this. I previously mentioned that in 2006, when my husband was diagnosed with leukemia, I had to set aside work on many of my goals and focus more intensively on my family. During this time, my bond with God became much stronger. I spoke to Him, prayed to Him, and clung to Him more than ever. My relationships with friends and family members took on new depth, as I depended on them more than ever. I was weak, and they were strong for me.

We continued to give to our charities and church. I attended church as regularly as my schedule permitted. But my goals of making strides in life, taking on new projects, working on new habits simply fell aside. And, that was okay.

At another time in my life, it was a series of joyous events, not tragedies that caused me to say "uncle" and set my plan aside for a period of time. In the space of one year, my son got married, my two married children each blessed us with a new grandson, my youngest son graduated from college, and my oldest son moved back to the states from Dubai. There were actually more events than these, but these were the big ones. So, I allowed myself a period of time when I deliberately set aside my plan and worked on only those components that I prioritized and had time for, knowing, because I have been at this for many years, that I would pick it up again.

And, that is the message of this section. Don't put your plan aside unless it is necessary. But know that at certain times in life, it is necessary to set your plan aside. When you can breathe again, dust off your plan, redo your goals, and move forward. That simple.

What is so important at these times is to know that God is still in charge. If you do believe, as I do, that all things that come to you pass through His hands, during these times of personal chaos, it is important to look for the lessons behind the events. What is God teaching me? What can I learn from this event?

And, if you don't believe that all things that come to you pass first through His hands, that things happen over which He chooses not to exert control, then ask Him for the strength to see you through these rough times and ask Him to show you how to use these events to become even more the person He designed you to be.

But, no matter what, and I know how hard this is—trust me—in all things, give Him thanks. Thanks for what He can accomplish within you when you are weak. Thanks for what He can accomplish through you for others when you are strong for them. Give thanks because ultimately, He is on the throne and He is in control. He will bring you through!

Chapter 12

Living Stones

I come from a family of pretty committed introverts. We like people, but only in small numbers and for limited periods of time. You can imagine, then, that I was very happy when I discovered that the man I married was also an introvert. So, even though we both had leadership roles in organizations, when we came home, we liked nothing better than to "nest".

But something happened when my husband had leukemia. As I mentioned earlier, he had to move away from home for many months while he completed his chemotherapy. Prior to this, he often said, "It would be nice to be able to go off somewhere for a period of time where I could just focus on my writing and painting." Well, not in the manner any of us wanted or expected, he got his wish. He moved into a home with his own room (he had to stay close to the hospital because the chemo drugs he was on nearly entirely eliminated his immune system, and he had to have immediate access to the emergency room if he ran a fever, developed a bad cold, etc.). Overall, he did well in between treatments. He set up his room with his writing materials and with his painting supplies. And, do you know what he found out? He needed people. In fact, he so missed being with people, he could only paint or write for short periods of time before he had to go out and socialize. Thankfully, we had developed a system to have family with him on a regular basis. And, the home he lived in was developed for cancer patients under treatment, so the center itself was a community! And, my husband thrived in that environment!

Why do I mention this in terms of goal setting and community? Because it is imperative for you to know that **you were designed for community**. Even if you have tendencies toward being an introvert, you need people — and in some ways, because you tend not to engage with other people as easily as extroverts, you need people even more. You seek out fewer social engagements, and so you are more likely to miss out on these important relationships — to share happiness, sorrow, need and plenty.

So, how does Branch Living relate to this innate need we have for community? In several ways:

1. Branch Living is best worked out in community – I discussed this in an earlier section, but it is worth repeating. Branch Living can be done on your own, and if you aren't part of a tight church group, Life Group, or group of similarly-minded friends, by all means, start the Branch Living process on your own. At the time I was developing the Branch Living process from years of doing individual and professional strategic planning, I did not have a close group of friends with whom I felt comfortable exploring this planning process. And so, I held myself accountable and moved ahead with my plan. However, the experience is much richer when you have a group of caring friends/ church members/life group members with whom you can share the journey. But, if need be, start on your own. If you follow these steps, soon you should find a group to join — or find friends whom you can engage in the process!

Those using the Branch Living system in groups can cheer each other along, challenge each other to keep pressing ahead, provide support when things aren't going well, and celebrate when stretch goals are realized.

If you cannot find an in-person group, by all means, join our online group and participate/ make friends/ get support. Who knows, it might lead you to form an in-person group!

2. The Apostle Peter states that we are the living stones (1 Peter 2:5) that form the Church—and each stone is important, regardless of where it is placed. We support each other, and we all contribute. So, please realize that you need the others in the Church—and they need you. And, we need you in the Branch Living community! You were created with unique gifts—and those gifts need to be shared. It is in the sharing of those gifts that you will find fulfillment.

The take aways?

1. You were made to live in community.

2. You are uniquely gifted.

3. Your gifts are meant to share.

4. You will benefit from access to the gifts of others.

Keep these points in mind as you refine your goals.

"Your people will rebuild the ancient ruins and will raise up the age-old foundations; YOU will be called Repairer of Broken Walls, Restorer of Streets with Dwellings." (Isaiah 58:12)

Chapter 13

Your Plan Belongs to God

The ultimate plan is God's plan. He is moving behind the scenes working to bring everyone into communion with Him. We can choose to open ourselves to Him and ask to be part of this amazing plan, and work with Him and others to play our part. But, ultimately, rest assured, God is in control.

There are times when we are working on our Branch Living plan, we hit a rough spot, and don't meet our goals. Often, we feel like failures. When these goals pertain to furthering our church or taking care of our families, we can feel demoralized.

It is tempting in these cases to get discouraged, throw up our hands, and quit. But, when we know that we can get up and try again, it is very reassuring. When we know that failing can make us much stronger for the next round, we can see that we can use failures to push us even further ahead. And, it is comforting to know that even if we fail, God's plan moves on.

I once heard a story about a quilter who was working on a beautiful quilt with her granddaughter. The child tried hard, but many of her stitches were large or crooked. But, her grandmother was a quilting pro. She knew how to take the less-than-perfect stitches of her granddaughter and incorporate them into the quilt so that the mistakes looked planned. And, as she incorporated the stiches into the overall design of the quilt, the grandmother knew that this was part of the process of how her granddaughter would become a fine quilter.

And, so it is with God. He knows we will fail. But He also knows that we have it within us to learn, move ahead, and succeed. So know that as you work your plan and you have failures, you are not messing up God's ultimate plan. He will work those failures into his overall scheme. The pattern might change a bit, but ultimately, the quilt will be of His making.

Isn't it a privilege to have been given the opportunity to contribute our stitches?

Chapter 14

Seasons: Lent

The music is not in the notes, but in the silence in between.
Wolfgang Amadeus Mozart

Lent is a wonderful, less celebrated season. It is the quieter, more reflective church season that is greatly overshadowed by the glitz and grandeur of Christmas.

There is nothing in the Bible that should make these seasons so distinctly different. If anything, the Bible would lead us to celebrate Easter more robustly. Christmas celebrates Jesus' birth — when the Light came into the world — definitely a moment to celebrate. Easter commemorates the day that Jesus rose from the dead, and opened the gates of heaven for you and for me. It is the fulfillment of His purpose for coming to earth. Without Easter, there is no Christianity. There is no hope.

But, the season leading up to Easter, Lent, is hardly even noted. Many of us go to church on Ash Wednesday (some following a raucous Fat Tuesday/ Mardi Gras celebration!), and receive communion. Often we participate in the Ceremony of the Ashes, when the minister makes a cross on our forehead or hand from the ashes, symbolizing the beginning of our period of repentance.

Some give up something during the Lenten season to remind them of the sacrifice that Christ made for them. This is how I began my journey into learning the beauty and richness of Lent.

Lent offers us much that our society devalues but which each of us, down deep in the depths of our soul, thirsts for.

In my journey of falling in love with Lent, I have found that, when richly celebrated, Lent gives us a chance to: slow down, reflect, sacrifice in a small way to be in touch in a big way, have a new start, break a bad habit, develop a good habit, seek our purpose, celebrate life's small gifts and small moments, take an account of our lives, think about our legacies, and/ or plan the rest of the year.

For these reasons, I find Lent to be the most meaningful and significant season of the year. It comes just at the time of the year when the frantic pace of Christmas is behind us. The decorations are all put away. The football season is behind us. So is Valentine's Day. It isn't spring quite yet. It isn't daylight savings time. It is still pretty dark in my part of the world. Really, it could be quite depressing. Except, there is Lent.

What role does Lent play in Branch Living? It is a time for second chances. Many people will engage in goals setting at first of the year. The new year, by its very name and nature, is a time of fresh starts and new beginnings. But, studies reveal that only eight percent of those who make a resolution at the first of the year will be successful in keeping that resolution.

Why is that?

I believe, and have experienced, that life simply gets in the way. New Year's comes right at the end of one of the busiest times on the calendar. I find that I always look forward to the new year. It is the last celebration of the season. It gives us a reason to continue the festivities for another week. I make my New Year's resolutions, and then what happens the next couple of weeks? I am busy catching up on all of life's obligations that were shelved during the Christmas season. I am putting away decorations, stripping the tree of its ornaments, getting the house cleaned up, gifts put away—whew! Now, what were those New Year's resolutions??

The beginning of the year is a wonderful opportunity for a fresh start. But, it occurs at a point of the year that is just too chaotic to have the time and the space to make change truly stick. But, then comes Lent. It comes in a period of quietness. So, instead of languishing in winter doldrums, I choose to drink all of the life and meaning out of Lent that I can.

Here is what I take from Lent—what Lent graciously gives to me. It offers the time and space needed to really allow Branch Living to infuse my life:

1. Slow Down

Lent is a wonderful time to move into slow motion after the rush of the Christmas and New Year's season. It is a time to hunker down and appreciate the fact that the world has become still, awaiting spring.

All of nature goes through a period of dormancy. It is a time to rest. A time to store up energy. A time to replenish.

Although most of us, myself included, still have many day-to-day responsibilities that never seem to completely go away, we can make a conscious effort to bring more solitude and a greater sense of calm into our days, especially the days of Lent.

To do this requires effort. The world will try to suck us into the stressful tempo that surrounds us. But, you can make an effort to disengage in several ways. Here are a few of the ways I have found to disengage during Lent:

Turn off the Television – this is one of the best and most effective ways to find time in your schedule. When you come home at night—or when others come home to you—turn off the television and put on soft music instead. Create a lovely space for creativity, thought, reflection, and gathering. Keep the noise of the world out of this season as much as possible.

Schedule time apart—make a conscious effort to schedule alone time. Following the Christmas rush, I go through my calendar and block off days and sections of days for time off. I use this time to really dive into the areas of my life that I may have neglected during that last week of the year. I give thoughtful reflection to the year ahead and what I want to accomplish in each of my Branch Living categories. I get ready to begin a fresh new way to do my Bible study and my devotions, each year changing it up a bit. I think about the organizations that I want to support this year with my time and talents. I schedule time to visit loved ones and block those dates in my schedule. I set up my time for my "New" and "Renew" goals. And, I think about the "habits" I want to continue to develop during the year. If I have found time at the beginning of the year for all of this planning, then I refresh, revitalize, and recommit to these goals. Lent is a time to take a first or second look, to get back on track, and to refine your Branch Living goals.

Pray more—sometime in this rather grey and uninspiring time of the year, God can seem very far away. This alone can make you feel less energized and inspired and a bit more apathetic. This is where "faith over feeling" has to kick in. We know that God is always close and never leaves us. We know that the Holy Spirit has been given to us as a comforter and guide. So, it behooves us to reach out more to God. If we feel more distant, we know He hasn't moved, so we need to take steps toward Him. Prayer is one of the most effective ways of doing this. Set aside time during your day to share your heart with God. Cast your cares and troubles on Him. Thank Him for the wonderful life He has given to you!

Fast—Fasting is a lost form of connecting deeply with God. Fasting does provided us time to slow down and focus. When we aren't troubled with food shopping, preparation, and clean up, we have more time to slow down and go deeper with God. Of course, you must be in good health and have no issues such as problems with blood sugar, etc. to fast. If you are at all in doubt, ask your health care professional. But, the combination of fasting for short periods of time and prayer is an incredibly effective way to power your way through the doldrums.

2. Reflect. We often get so accustomed to looking forward, that we don't look at the past or the present. It is good, from time to time, to take inventory of what the previous year brought to us and where we stand with all of the various components of our life. I like to go through the various Branch Living components and do a mental inventory of what took place last year, where I currently am with things, and where I feel I should go during the coming year. These times of reflection can open up opportunities for praise, petitions, and confession.

3. Sacrifice in a small way to be in touch in a big way—for me, this opened the door to my deeper understanding of Lent. When I was younger, I used to give up something—soda, chocolate—something simple but something I loved. I would spend the season of Lent lamenting that I didn't have the little treat—and looking forward to an Easter gorge. Not a pretty picture, I confess. But, back then, the small thing that I gave up, which normally I would not think about, became a constant needling source of aggravation. Needless to say, Lent was not a time in which I went deeper in my faith. It was a time when I felt sorry for myself.

That all changed when I decided to give up something for Lent that I needed to give up: my angry nature. I could feel anger seeping into my day. It was a very subtle seep—not an earth shattering personality change. Just a burning I would feel during the day, followed by an outburst or two. I felt unhappy about it. I felt like I didn't want to be the angry person I was slowly becoming. But, I felt helpless to change. But, then came Lent. I could give up chocolate. I could give up television. But, could I give up an angry nature? Why not give it a try?

And so, every day, as that slow burn would start within my nature, I would pause, pray and give it over to God. I wish I could tell you that on the first day of Lent, all of my anger was gone. That is simply not the case. But, the pattern began. Stop. Pray. Give it to God. One day. And then the next day. And the next. I told no one, not even my husband, that I had given up anger for Lent. This was between God and me.

About two months into this pattern (yes—post Lent), my husband and I were working together in our kitchen, and he turned to me and said, "You know, for some reason, you seem so much less angry than you used to." I was shocked. My gosh, it showed. Thank God (literally), Lent worked when nothing else had. Who knew? That quiet in between time of year could be just the time for small miracles.

Before this, what I gave up for Lent contributed to the darkness of that in between time. But, when I decided to use Lent as a time to sacrifice in a small way to gain in a big way, Lent unfolded to me like a flower in May. And, it has ever since.

In the next section of the book, we will look at the importance of gratefulness to Branch Living, but it was during Lent that I learned that lesson as well. During the Lenten season following the year in which I had given over my angry nature to God, I tried to decide what to give up. I landed, instead, on what to incorporate: thankfulness! In a sense, you could say that I decided to give up not being thankful.

But how to become more thankful? In this particular year, I decided to spend the season of Lent writing a thank you card every day to someone whom I was grateful to have in my life. I wrote each note, mentioning something specific that I was thankful for concerning each person. At first, I must admit, it was difficult. I was out of the thankfulness habit. But as each day progressed, it actually became easier. One thought of thankfulness led to another. Soon, I was looking forward to the next thank you note, throughout the season.

Just think, there are so many ways to start to develop thankfulness during this season: vow to take a moment every day to be appreciative for something or someone in your life, especially the simple things. Thankful for steaming cups of coffee. For the first song of the peepers. For the stars that blanket the sky. One by one, name the things that surround you that you typically just walk by.

Another way to develop thankfulness is to create a "thankful journal" in which each day, you record several things for which you are thankful. Leave the journal in a conspicuous place so that you can easily record your observations or so that you can pick it up and remind yourself of all you have to be grateful for.

Make small sacrifices to achieve big gains. If you give up something special to you, something that makes a difference in your day, be it your morning cup of coffee, your glass of wine with dinner, your chocolate splurge at the end of the day, do it with the intention of being "in the spirit of Lent."

4. Make a new start. Sometimes the New Year's season is just too busy for a new start. Lent offers that "let's try this again" approach, especially for those areas of your life that require more self-introspection and reflection. Take this time to "let the Spirit work in you" to help you discover the areas in your life that need work and care.

5. Break a bad habit. Perhaps your soul searching revealed a habit you needed to address, much as I had to address my problem with anger. Lent offers the perfect opportunity to take on these types of challenges! Often, discovering and rooting out undesirable behaviors takes time and introspection. Sometimes, we can't see or don't want to admit to ourselves the negative, destructive habits or behaviors that we most need to change to have a richer, more Christ-centered life. If you have someone in your life who truly wants what is best for you and whom you trust, you can reach out to that person and ask, "If you could name one thing in my life which I could change that would most enhance my walk with Christ and my witness to my faith, what would that be?" Again, you have to have a pretty intimate relationship with someone for that person to feel comfortable giving you that type of perspective and for you to receive it in the right light. Otherwise, this type of discussion could be a relationship breaker. If you do venture down this pathway, be prepared to thank the person for their candid advice, no matter how shocked you might be or how much it might hurt your pride. But, don't automatically accept this perception of your character until you examine it and it rings true to you. If you see that is true and want to change it, Lent presents the season for such changes. But, how do you make such a change?

Here are a few tips I have used: first, acknowledge the imperfection and ask God to forgive you for allowing it to take root in your life. Next, forgive yourself. You might be tempted to wallow in self-pity and regret, but why? You are putting this behind you now. As the Christian song, "Tell Your Heart to Beat Again" reminds us, "you don't live there anymore." Once you ask for forgiveness and pledge to move ahead, you are walking away from that trait, not allowing it to hold on to you like a ball and chain. Lastly, each time you find yourself tempted to engage in whatever bad behavior you are disposing of, take a breath, acknowledge to yourself that you have set this aside—that that trait no longer defines who you are. Say a prayer, and move on. Soon, this will become your new habit. And, the time when you engage in the behavior will be less and less frequent.

6. Develop a good habit. Just as it is hard to weed out a bad behavior, it is equally hard to root a good behavior. Studies have shown that it takes a full 66 days to develop a good habit—longer than the season of Lent, but Lent should get you most of the way there! Good habits, such as thankfulness, fill the voids that the removal of bad habits leave us with. So, in addition to discovering your less desirable traits, concentrate too on the good traits you would like to "grow." A good place to start is with the fruits of the Spirit, which are God-given, but which can be cultivated once the seeds are planted. These fruits are: love, joy, peace, long-suffering, gentleness, goodness, and faith. When I seek to be "good soil" for the seeds of these fruits, I ask myself, "What does a person who is____ (fill in the blank with one of the attributes) do in this situation?" And, then, I try to emulate those I know who exemplify this trait.

There is a woman in our church who, to me, is the epitome of gentleness. I have never heard her raise her voice. I have never heard her say an unkind word about anyone, even those whom I might think "deserve" an unkind word or two. So, when I am tempted to gossip or think unkindly of someone else, and I realize that I am not exhibiting this gentle spirit, I often think of this woman and ask myself, "How would Sarah (not her name) act in this situation?" and then I try to behave in the same manner. Often, it is just a matter of smiling and keeping my mouth firmly shut!

So, look at the seeds of good habits that are not taking root in your life. Examine how you might cultivate traits that would elevate others and expand the witness of your faith.

7. Seek your purpose. There a few fortunate people in the world who have a full understanding of what they were put on this earth to do from a very early age. When I was growing up, I had a neighbor who never took a piano lesson in her life, but she played beautifully. She told me that when she heard a piece of music, she would sit down and play it. The arrangement of the sounds just

made sense to her. She used that gift to entertain people back in the 1950s and continued to pick out a piece of music for her neighbors from time to time.

I read an autobiography of an author who, from a very young age, would write short stories that his friends and teachers found to be "noteworthy." As an adult, he has won many awards for his novels. He feels that this gift was given to him at an early age and that he has simply cultivated it each day.

But, there are many of us who did not have this type of revelation at an early age. In fact, there are many people who will come to the end of their lives and only by looking back will have a sense of what their purpose was. And, there are those who will go to their graves never knowing and will have to wait for heaven to have a complete sense of "what that was all about!"

As Christians, we know that our purpose centers on serving God and His Kingdom. We each have a different and distinct role to implement His plan on earth. But how do we know what that is?

Many Christian writers have indicated that we are given unique talents and gifts to share with others here on earth. They suggest you look at those things you are good at—those things that come easily to you. I agree with this assessment. But, the beauty of Lent is that by examining yourself in terms of aspects of your character that you want to root out and others that you want to cultivate, you might also make some self-discoveries that have been buried over time. Perhaps as you are trying to become a more giving person, you will discover that you have a love of helping others that had somehow gotten buried over time. Lent is a great time for "going deeper" which can have the side benefit of self-discovery.

8. Celebrate small gifts and small moments. Life is lived primarily in the "ordinary." I touched upon the need to notice the small graces around us as we go through life in the section of being thankful. We can best do this by being present in the present moment. I have to remind myself of this on an ongoing basis. I am

training myself to take a mental picture of moments in life that I want to remember. Watching sunsets with my husband. Walking through our town listening to an amazing book on tape. Seeing the tulip magnolia in full bloom outside of our kitchen window. So many snapshots that pass so quickly. I try to hold onto them by noting how they impact all of my senses: the smell, the look, the feel of it all. It is hard, at least it is hard for me, to stay in the moment, but it is so important, because the moment is gone all too soon.

9. Take account of your life. Lent provides the time to take a step back and evaluate your life in terms of where you are and where you thought you would be/ like to be. This can be a rather humbling experience but one that is very valuable, especially if you are at a point in your life when you feel you are simply drifting. Meditate on where you wanted to be as an adult when you were younger. Are you there? Do you still want to go there? If so, why haven't you made progress toward this vision? If not, why not? What have you learned or experienced that has taken you in a new direction? And exactly what is that direction? Too often as adults we are afraid to delve deeply into these thoughts because we uncover raw spots. It can be painful to remember dreams that have died, hopes that have been put aside, and opportunities that were not taken. But, it is important to review each of these areas for several reasons. First, unfulfilled hopes and dreams can create an unwanted anchor on our lives. We start to dream a new dream, and our subconscious tells us, "No, don't explore that. Remember you tried something like this before and you failed."

But, as Christians, two of our greatest attributes are hope and faith. We have to examine our failures and develop a good understanding of what went wrong. We then have to learn what we can from these dreams and goals that were not realized, make a conscious decision about whether we want to revisit them, and if not, we take our lessons from them and move on. We do not let them define us; we let them refine us for the dreams that lie ahead.

10. Think about your legacy. The time for deeper reflection that Lent provides also provides us with the time to consider, when we come to the end of our days, what type of legacy we want to leave to those who love us. This type of reflection can have profound results.

I remember an elderly woman who had been an alcoholic from her 20s all the way through her early 50s. Her life changed the day she found a lump in her breast that her doctor confirmed was breast cancer. She realized that she didn't really fear death. What she feared was the memories she would be leaving to her children and grandchildren of the type of person she had become. With her diagnosis, she was determined to become the woman she wanted to be remembered as during the rest of her life, even if her those remaining days were short. She had surgery for her breast cancer and entered rehab for her alcohol addiction. She pledged to each of her children to be the mother she had not been for them when they were young and to be a grandmother to their children whom they would be proud of.

And, she was good to her word. She never drank alcohol again. She spent time individually with each of her children. She hosted big family events at her white frame farmhouse. She attended church every Sunday. She reprioritized her life, and even this late in life, it had a major impact on her children and on her grandchildren. They called her "beloved" in spite of the many years when she disappointed them. She changed the legacy she left behind. When she died, she had been sober for nearly 40 years. Few remembered the "old" her – they remembered the devoted mother and grandmother. They remembered the family events at the farmhouse. They remembered the many times she helped out at the church. They remembered her deep and abiding faith.

What legacy do you plan to leave behind? It is never too late to leave the legacy you would like to leave behind. It is never too late to make a new start. Lent is a great time to make that decision to move forward on the track you want to be on.

11. Plan the rest of the year. As you reflect on the direction you want to take with your life, you can either reexamine or begin developing your Branch Living goals and plan for the year ahead. If you began the Branch Living program at the beginning of the year, now is a good time to reevaluate the goals and continue to move ahead, refining the goals as needed/ desired. If you began your Branch Living program and fell away for a period of time, now is a good time to pick your plan back up, dust it off and make the changes you need to move ahead.

Perhaps you set goals that were too lofty and when you failed to meet your targets, you quit set the whole plan aside. That is understandable. Often, when we start to set goals, we get carried away, and then real life reminds us of how little time we truly have in our days. We get discouraged and scrap our plans all together. But, Lent provides us with the opportunity to reevaluate, dust off old plans, and begin again.

Lent is the time for reflection, realizing our need for our Savior because we cannot do life on our own. It is the time to come to grips with our weaknesses, things which need to be removed from our life and things that need to be added to our life to be more in tune with our faith.

It is the time to prepare to get back on track, because after Lent…Easter comes.

Chapter 15

Seasons: Easter

*Do not abandon yourselves to despair. We are the Easter
people and hallelujah is our song.*
Pope John Paul II

Easter is the greatest gift our Father has ever given. It is the gift of His Son, who took the sins of those who believe in Him to the grave, and opened the doors to heaven to those who trust Him to be their Savior. Nothing compares. Nothing ever will. We are made new through Him.

Easter shows us that death does not hold the final card. He does. And that lesson plays out in many ways in our life.

God can revitalize lives that seem dead. God can bring a new spark to old dreams. God can bring life where others only see death.

"He is risen; he is not here."
Mark 16:6

After the time of reflection, repentance, examination, and planning, Easter comes with its rebirth and renewal.

Easter brings JOY. And, we should let that Joy permeate all we are and all we do.

"If you keep my commandments, you remain in my love' just as I have kept my Father's commands and remain in his love. I have told you this so that my joy may be in you and that your joy may be complete."
John 15:10-11

That is the most important part of Branch Living: sharing the Joy and Love of Christ to an oftentimes sad and lonely world.

Go back through your goals. Remember, they should not be burdensome. If you have set down too aggressive of a plan, pare it back to a more reasonable and achievable course.

"Take my yoke upon you and learn from me, for I am gentle and humble in heart, and you will find rest for your souls. For my yoke is easy and my burden is light."
Matthew 11:29 and 30

You should reevaluate your goals and ensure that they are ambitious but not overwhelming. If you get discouraged, you will not reflect the love and joy of Christ to the world. Set your goals to be realistic. Set your pathway so that you will continue to experience the Joy of Christ not only on Easter Day but also throughout the year.

Remember the "B" in Branch Living is the first and foundational goal of Branch Living, and that is your Bond with God. Honor it first and foremost. If you need to set other goals aside from time to time, that is understandable. But, keep your time with God at the forefront. By doing this, you will not fail. You will enjoy the richness and the joy of Branch Living. And, you will keep the message of Easter in your heart throughout the year. He reigns!

Chapter 16

Seasons: Pentecost

One of the most neglected church holy days is Pentecost. Pentecost celebrates the day when the Holy Spirit came down on the apostles forty days after Easter.

When the day of Pentecost came, they were all together in one place. Suddenly a sound like the blowing of a violent wind came from heaven and filled the whole house where they were sitting. They saw what seemed to be tongues of fire that separated and came to rest on each of them. All of them were filled with the Holy Spirit and began to speak in tongues as the Spirit enabled them.
Acts 2: 1-4

The Holy Spirit is what empowered the apostles to take the Good News of the Gospel out to all of the world. For this reason, many consider Pentecost to be the birthday of the church. While many American Christians tend not to celebrate Pentecost, traditional European churches consider it to be a major feast day. In

Germany, there are only three national holidays that span two days: Christmas, Easter, and Pentecost.

Originally, Pentecost was a Jewish holiday that was held 50 days after Passover. It celebrated thankfulness for harvested crops. And, the bounty that the Spirit provides to all believers, in a sense, is a bountiful harvest.

So, how does Pentecost impact Branch Living? It provides us with the fire we need to change our lives and fulfill our purpose; it moves us to tune into the Holy Spirit and pray for revival; it adds fervency to our prayer lives for our world, our nation, and each other; and it causes us to fall in love, all over again, with Christ.

Pentecost makes what Christ did "real." When we read and reread the stories pertaining to Christ's life, we have a tendency to become cold to them. They lose all of the emotional undertones because they simply become too familiar.

Pentecost provides us with the fiery love of God for all He loves. This empowers us to live our lives to the fullest in service to Him. It gives us the strength to persevere. It gives us the passion to live our lives as ambassadors of the King we serve to those who do not know Him.

Pentecost comes at a time of the church year when it is needed the most. It follows the flurry and joy of Christmas, the reflective time of Lent, the newness and "awestruck wonder" of Easter. And then what? The passion and the fire of Pentecost. It is what gave the disciples the power to preach the Word to all corners of the earth. It is what gives you the power to live this life in fullest service to Him.

Paul Stewart, the lead pastor at The Gateway Church in Des Moines, states:

The truth of Jesus Christ does not bring power. It does not result in power. It does not lead to power. It is the power.

The baptism of the Holy Spirit is when you experience the truth of the gospel to such a degree that your whole heart and mind and body are filled with it.

Greg Laurie, pastor of the Harvest Christian Fellowship, in his blog, puts it like this:

Alfred Nobel, the founder of the Nobel Peace Prize, also was the man who created dynamite. When he came up with this new explosive kind of technology, he needed a name. So he spoke with a friend who knew the Greek language well and asked him what the Greek word for "explosion" was. That word was dunamis, and so Nobel named his invention "dynamite."

When the apostle Paul wrote in Romans 1:16, "For I am not ashamed of the gospel of Christ, for it is the power of God to salvation for everyone who believes," the word "power" is translated from that same Greek word: "dunamis."

Clearly, when the Holy Spirit came down on the people during Pentecost, this was dunamis — dynamite.

So, what can we do to fully embrace Pentecost?

Pope Francis recently shed light on our personal pathway to Pentecost. He said, "Without prayer, there is no place for the Holy Spirit. Ask God to send us this gift: "Lord, give us the Holy Spirit so that we may discern at all times what we have to do.'" It is through the Holy Spirit, he added, that Christians can see the truth. Therefore he encouraged Christians to pray for this grace and to follow what the Spirit asks.

"The progress of the Church," says Pope Francis, "is the work of the Holy Spirit, which makes us listen to the voice of the Lord." "How can I make sure that voice I hear is the voice of Jesus," asked Pope Francis, "that what I feel I have to do is done by the Holy Spirit? The answer is by praying."

Praying for power and the guidance of the Holy Spirit is the key to unlocking the power of Pentecost all year long. If you have ever lit a small fire and wanted it to grow in strength and power, what do you do? You blow on the fire to bring it to a stronger flame. Prayer is that breath.

The Holy Spirit can bring the power of Pentecost into our daily lives as well. I have served in leadership roles in hospitals for more than twenty-five years. When you serve prominent community organizations, you are, from time to time, wrongly accused of having motives you do not have or of taking actions that you have not taken. When I react defensively, I find that I am angry or hurt. When I pray for the Holy Spirit to guide my response, I find that I don't react, I respond. And, the difference, the pause to turn to the Holy Spirit's power and not my own, changes everything.

As popular pastor Charles Stanley states, in these circumstances we must pray for spiritual discernment, a quiet spirit, and wisdom. The Holy Spirit can show us how to approach our accuser and see beyond hurtful words or actions. A quiet spirit allows us to quiet our natural human reaction to defend ourselves. And, wisdom puts a seal on our lips, allowing the Holy Spirit to show us what to say and when.

This is just one example of what the power of the Spirit living in us can do for us and for those around us. And, it is all accessed through prayer.

Pentecost power is released daily through our active prayer life. Pentecost serves as the reminder to the church and to each of us to unlock that power daily.

Chapter 17

Seasons: Christmas

Our current culture promotes the busyness, lavishness, and "over-the-topness" of Christmas. The brighter, bigger, and busier the Christmas—the better the time was had by all. But, here is the dirty little secret of Christmas. You will never be able to have a Christmas that is bright enough, big enough or busy enough to fill the void that the real Christmas can fill. There is only one way Christmas can fill our hearts, and that is through simplicity, quietness, reflection and peace. Our culture tells us to live Christmas large and outside of ourselves. Christmas tells us to live Christmas small and to move inside ourselves for the experience.

We don't listen. I don't listen—often. But, Christmas has always held this message for us. Our culture says that kings are born in elaborate palaces. Christmas says true kings are born in stables. The world tells us that the greatest gifts are expensive. Christmas tells us that the greatest gifts are submitted lives and open hearts.

Our society tells us that Christmas involves four weeks of "doing it all." Christmas, instead, reveals a slow, steady walk of faith.

Because of these polar opposites tug at us during this holy time of year, I recommend taking a slow and steady walk toward the "true" Christmas, and weaning ourselves slowly from the cultural tug of Christmas. Notice that I did not say to abandon our cultural traditions of Christmas — for most of us, that would make Christmas too alien from how we have always experienced it. If you and your family can go "cold turkey" and enter the true spirit of Christmas in one swoop, I think that is great. But, for many of us, cold turkey doesn't work. It is easier for us to "walk it back."

There is nothing morally wrong with brightly decorated trees, presents, and parties. In fact, they add joy to a rather dark time of year. And, the cultural Christmas does have strong commonality with the true spirit of Christmas. This includes family gatherings, sending warm wishes to loved ones, the spirit of peace and joy, Christmas Eve worship, and shining light into a darkened world. These connecting points provide us a means to get back in step with the real Christmas, while still enjoying the culture of Christmas we have created.

Here are tips to get us back on the path to the heart-filling Christmas we long for:

1. Bring to mind what your heart craves from Christmas. We fall in love with Christmas each year because of the promise of peace, joy, love and goodwill toward all men. God loves us so much, that He put his own power and glory on the shelf, came down and became a tiny vulnerable baby who would grow to show us the right way to live our lives. This amazing love is the true force of Christmas, and it is what our hearts long for. Time with God to hear His amazing love story as though we had not heard it before. Time to allow that amazing love to permeate our souls. Time to share that love with those around us. This is what our heart craves from Christmas.

2. Take care of as many Christmas activities as possible before the season begins. If possible purchase and wrap your gifts, decorate

your house, both inside and out, and get your cards ready to mail before December. This requires real discipline and requires that you schedule time to get this done. But, if you want to experience the true Christmas, you must create space, time, and peace in your schedule for it to occur.

3. Fill your schedule with the events and activities that put you in the true spirit of Christmas. They include many of the components of Branch Living – time to bond with God, time for relationships, time to donate your time and talent (alms), time to become new/ renew our world.

4. Give yourself a slowed down approach this month. Don't press yourself to make progress on your goals. Take life at a bit slower pace this month to give yourself needed room. If you normally exercise five days per week, and you need to cut back to three days per week to give yourself more time for drinking in the season, do it. Focus this month on the first three aspects of Branch Living—time with God (Bonding), Relationships, and Alms. Cut back on the new/ renew aspects of your plan and the habits, if need be. They will be waiting for you in the next chapter of this book, the year, and of your life—New Year's!

Chapter 18

Seasons: A New Year

A new year offers us a big clean slate. In fact, each new day offers us this same clean slate, if we would choose to see life in that way. But, as a culture, we see the new year as an opportunity to start fresh.

To fully take advantage of this opportunity for a fresh start, we need to clean the slate. How do we do this?

I find that the period of time after Christmas and before the new year offers a wonderful spot to pause and prepare for the new year ahead. As I mentioned in an earlier chapter, the new year can often be so busy so as not to be a good time to start the new year of Branch Living. Some find it better to start a week into the new year, or even later, at Lent or Easter. But, most of us like the thought of having New Year's resolutions, and Branch Living is designed to bring these heartfelt resolutions to life—to give them good soil and to help them root. So if you elect to start your new

Branch Living year at the beginning of the new year, here are some tips to help you get started.

Use the week before new year to reflect, set new goals, reevaluate your current/ prior goals, and start your new plan.

1. Reflect—this is the best way to clean the slate for a new year. Plato and Socrates have each been credited with stating that "an unexamined life is not worth living." Though this is a rather severe statement, I believe that the essence of it is true. Human beings are the only living beings that can be consciously reflective. Other creatures are victims of conditioning and instinct—and we are too. But, we have the higher level of thinking that allows us to move ahead of our instincts and make conscious decisions as to how we want our lives to be different. This is the best way of creating a clean slate. Reflect on the past and consciously set a new course.

If you are starting Branch Living for the first time, reading this book will give you good insight into how to set your goals for daily living and how to schedule your time to effectively live out your goals. If you just completed a year of Branch Living and are preparing to begin a new plan for this new year, ask yourself these questions concerning each of your goals.

a) Was I successful in achieving what I set out to do?
b) If so, what helped me be successful? How can I apply this success to my other goals?
c) If I was not successful in this area, what stood in my way of success? How can I overcome these barriers? How can I keep these barriers from occurring in other areas of my life?
d) Did I complete this goal? Did I reward myself in some way to celebrate my success?
e) Did I not complete this goal? Do I need to renew or refresh this goal in some way? Are there lessons or small achievements I should celebrate concerning making meaningful progress on this goal?

Write down your thoughts for each of you goals. This is the basis of your new year of Branch Living.

2. Set new goals and reevaluate your current/ prior goals — in light of your reflections:

a) What goals will you carry forward into the following year?
b) How can you structure them to overcome any difficulties you experienced last year? Were you too aggressive? Do you need to scale the goal back a bit? Do you need to put a new twist on this goal?
c) What new goals do you need to set to achieve the renewed life you seek — the one God is working with you to bring to life? The one He envisioned for you from the very start?

3. Start your new plan, go back to the beginning of this book and start reading it now with new eyes, develop your new plans. Branch Living should be new and renewed each and every year — or more often if you fall off course midyear. Remember — you never fail — you just fall, pick yourself up, dust yourself off, and begin anew!

Consider attending a Branch Living retreat. Go to our website BranchLiving.org to find the retreat nearest to you. Don't see one? Let us know you are interested, and we will see if we can plan a retreat in your area.

That life you want? It is waiting out there for you. Start walking – or running — toward it!

Forward!

Chapter 19

Tips for When You Struggle

If you start to feel discouraged in your goal keeping, here are some tips to keep you going:

1. Failure or backsliding is not a permanent state—you always have the next day to start fresh! If you are in the middle of the month and want to pick things back up, simply cut your goals in half for the month and move on. Don't let yesterday's failures hinder you from tomorrow's successes! Forward!

2. Remember—one move forward can lead to the next—don't stop taking small steps even when you don't have the energy to take big ones. Sometimes when I don't feel like writing, I will tell myself, "Just sit down and write one page. You don't have to do anything more than one page, and then you can turn off the computer." What I find is that once I write one page, the next page comes rather easily, and then the next. Nine times out of ten, I find the interest and energy to just keep going. Getting started is the

hard part. Science teaches us that it take far more energy to put something into motion than to keep it there.

3. Learn the system – set big goals and work backward – this is the key to the process of Branch Living in a nutshell. If you learn the system, you can easily pick up where you left off. You need at least one or two BIG goals in life to motivate you and keep you going. It doesn't matter if it takes you longer to realize those goals – or if those goals did not work out, but they led you to new goals. Keep plugging along, and don't get discouraged! Enjoy the journey as you make progress.

4. Don't let difficulties stop you – look at them for what they are, bumps in the road. Few if any endeavors go flawlessly. When you start out, expect from the very beginning that you will encounter problems along the way, so you aren't surprised when you come up against them. "So there you are!" you say to yourself, and then you find a way to move forward or around the circumstance. But, don't give up.

5. If you work Monday- Friday, schedule you time for Branch Living primarily on weekends – with the exception of Bible study, family, devotions, and diet and exercise, most of your plans can hold off until Friday night through Sunday night. That includes your giving of time and money, catching up on your various relationships, your new and renewed projects, and many of your "habits." I have worked outside of the home for more than 30 years, and I know how difficult it is to schedule time to make progress on goals when you get home at six at night and still need to make and eat dinner, clean up, tidy the house, and get ready for the next day. If you can make time for your Bible study, exercise, devotions, and family, you are doing an awesome job! If you can squeeze out time for additional progress on goals, great. But, don't sacrifice your family, sleep or sanity! Thankfully, even in the busiest of families (and we are a pastor's family with three kids), you can generally find time on the weekend to make real progress on your goals.

6. Schedule "time off" from your goals to regenerate/ relax/ think—sometimes you want to take a few weekends off as well. Go ahead! Work these weekends into your schedule so that you don't fall behind, and then ENJOY that time off. I find that when I do take a "goal holiday," I come back refreshed and ready to start again. And, on occasion, my mind is free during those breaks to think of new ways of achieving the goals I have. Often times, when we are away for a weekend, my husband and I will start talking about one of our projects, and the discussion leads us into directions that neither of us had considered, all because the pressure of other obligations is off of our shoulders for a period of time.

7. Have Fun! Be Optimistic!—we each have so much to be grateful for. If we took a detailed inventory of all of our blessings, we would spend the rest of our lives writing them down! Joy is ours through Christ—and nothing can take that away from us! So, have fun with Branch Living! Take a positive approach! Good things are coming your way! Laugh often and enjoy the ride!

8. Don't Give Up!—reach out to others, but be determined within yourself that you are going to work with God to make a difference in yourself and in the world. Branch Living is a system, a valuable tool, and a network of support. You need to be positive, centered, prayerful, and determined!

"Bear in mind that your own resolution to succeed is more important than any other."
Abraham Lincoln

Chapter 20

Gratitude

That is our greatest gift to our Savior: a life well lived, according to His guidance, as a daily act of appreciation.

Remember, daily acts of kindness and goodness to those who have no way of repaying us is a wonderful way of showing our gratitude to God.

For I was hungry and you gave me something to eat, I was thirsty and you gave me something to drink, I was a stranger and you invited me in, I needed clothes and you clothed me, I was sick and you looked after me, I was in prison and you came to visit me.'

"Then the righteous will answer him, 'Lord, when did we see you hungry and feed you, or thirsty and give you something to drink? When did we see you a stranger and invite you in, or needing clothes and clothe you? When did we see you sick or in prison and go to visit you?'

"The King will reply, 'Truly I tell you, whatever you did for one of the least of these brothers and sisters of mine, you did for me.'
Matthew 25: 35-40

There is a challenge you can give yourself to help you to remember to express gratitude throughout your day. It is a tool that is often taught to managers and it goes like this: place ten pennies in your right pocket. Throughout your day, say thank you to those who work for you, give compliments, give assistance. Each time you say or do something for another person, move one of the pennies from your right pocket to your left. Never let a day go by without emptying your right pocket.

This same guidance could be given to us on how we give daily offerings to God, by our kind words and deeds to those around us from whom we have nothing to benefit. Try this: put ten pennies in your right hand pocket. Go throughout the day, holding the door for someone, sending a card to someone who is ill or lonely, making a meal for a shut in, telling someone how nice they look, giving a child a hug. Give these small, sincere, gifts to others as if you are giving them to God. Because, as you give to those who are in need, you do give to Him. And you honor Him.

Branch Living gives you the tools to give your life as an offering back to Him. There is no life better lived than this!

At a worship service I recently attended, the question was asked, "What if you awoke tomorrow with only those things/ people/ circumstances for which you gave thanks today?" Think about it. If you could only carry into tomorrow those things you gave thanks for today, how many wonderful blessings would you leave behind for the lack of thankfulness? Even simple things. A baby's giggle. The pink light of early morning. The smell of coffee. Your loved one's face.

"Hem you blessings with thankfulness so they don't unravel."
Anonymous

"The unthankful heart discovers no mercies but let the thankful heart sweep through the day and as the magnet finds iron, so it will find, in every man, some heavenly blessings!"
Henry Ward Beecher

Chapter 21

Time

This is one lesson I wish I had learned much earlier in life. There are different ways to view time, and the subtle difference between them can make all the difference in how you spend your life.

The Greeks had two words for time: Chronos, which is quantitative time—seconds, minutes, hours. It is how many of us measure time, especially those of us who are tied to our to do lists and our schedules. We love to check things off of the list and move on to the next accomplishment. There is a sense of achievement, a feeling of accomplishment, in checking off what you have on the calendar or to do list and starting with a blank sheet for the next day. Americans are very centered on Chronos.

But, the Greeks also had a term for the quality of time: Kairos. Kairos is a bit harder to define because it is often interpreted differently. The definition I like is that it is the perfect time. Like when an apple is perfectly ripe. It has nothing to do with chronology. It has to do with the fullness of time. The perfect moment in time.

These are the rich moments you look back and say, "It all started when…." Some define Kairos as those moments when God steps in or which God had selected to further His purpose, and certainly those are Kairos moments. But certainly smaller moments exist that can only be measured in quality and not quantity. I am going to take a bit of liberty with the term, and say that in our day-to-day lives, Kairos moments are those moments that are unexpected and ultimately add tremendously to the quality of our lives — not the quantity.

When a new friend walks into your life. When you take a moment to visit that church you had heard about, and now you are surrounded in its beauty and warmth. When you go for a walk at night and look up at the sky, and the stars seem so bright you feel you could touch them. These moments are ripe, complete, and perfect. They cannot be measured in clock time. They can only be measured in heart time.

It is so important, as you are living your life to its fullest through Branch Living, not to turn into a list checker. Branch Living is not a method. It is not a guide to how to live your life. It is a pathway, and on any pathway, there are times you stop walking and look around. You set aside where you had planned to go and take a brief detour. There are moments that are more important than anything you have planned, and so your plans should be set aside, and you should enter the moment. Do this. You have not harmed your plan — you have set it aside instead to take advantage of this completely perfect moment. You have made the better choice.

Use your time wisely. Put yourself in the way of Kairos moments. Branch Living will bring focus and purpose to your time. But, don't stick so closely to the plan that you miss those memorable "Oh Wow!" moments.

Chapter 22

Staying In Touch

We need to support each other on this journey! I am so grateful that the Internet exists and has provided us with the ability to keep in touch with people from all across the globe.

We live in wonderful times, when we can locate old friends and make new friends who may live thousands of miles away. I have developed a website, blog, and Twitter account so that we can stay in touch. Please visit our website BranchLiving.org to meet others who are participating in Branch Living! There, you can read what others are doing, post your reflections of your journey, find out about upcoming events, email me, or just follow along! Look us up! I would love to have you stop by often!

Also, please keep an eye out for Branch Living training sessions that are offered around the country. If you would like to host one of these sessions, send me an email. If you would like to participate in a session, go to our website and learn how to sign up. If you would like to participate in a session, but don't see one scheduled close to where you live, email me, and I will let you know if plans are underway for a session near you!

Stay tuned for upcoming conferences where those who have joined the Branch Living family can meet face-to-face, share tips and encouragement!

We are seeking Branch Living Coaches to help keep the Branch Living groups moving ahead and well supported after the Branch Living retreats are over. Coaching helps us move beyond hearing the messages of Branch Living to absorbing it and making it part of your life. Statistics show that training is best absorbed in small pieces, with coaching. A 1997 study of 31 sector managers by Olivero, Bane, and Kopelman found that a training program increased productivity by 28%. But, when adding follow-up coaching to the training, productivity increased by 88%. Coaches help you reflect on what you are learning. They help keep Branch Living top-of-mind. As HighFlyingDivas.com states, "Learning and changing behaviors takes time and energy to become second nature. It is difficult to remember all that you have learned in a training course when you get back (to your routine) and fall back into the hectic routine."

The coaches we seek are respected in their circle (church, community). They are Christ-centered. They believe in the authority of the Bible. They believe in the skills taught through Branch Living, and they lead Branch Living groups by example. They are trusted, have direct conversations, and demonstrate humility and compassion. They come along side of us, put their arm around our shoulders, and say, "I know how that is. Here are some tips that might help."

If you are interested in serving as a coach, please contact us through our website.

We are constantly seeking to improve our Branch Living guide. If you see areas where we can improve, please contact us. Also, please share your stories with us. Stories breathe real life into abstract ideas. We all like to read how someone has taken a program, made it their own, and brought life to the ideas. We will be sharing these stories, with permission, on our website, so please visit often.

Conclusion: Singing a Love Song

The Bible is not just history. It is a crazy, roundabout story about the love of God for man, and the imperfect love we have for God. Each of our lives amounts to just that: a love song, good or bad, happy or tragic, to God. Our lives "sing" to Him as He continues to sing over us, each day, every day of His tremendous love for us.

Our lives sing to others. They sing of what resides in our hearts. Of our hopes and fears, of our courage or lack of strength. Of our trust in God. Of our disappointment and lack of faith in Him. Each day, every moment, we are singing out to each other and to our wonderful God.

What does your song say?

Jesus tells us that the first and greatest commandment is to "Love the Lord your God with all you heart and with all your soul and with all your mind." (Matthew 22:37) Not part way. Not most of the time. The commandment (not the request) is to love God completely with all of our heart, soul, and mind. This is the refrain of your song.

Jesus goes on to tell us the second commandment, "Love your neighbor as yourself." (Matthew 22:39)These are the stanzas of the song.

Jesus concludes by stating that "All of the Law and Prophets hang on these two commandments." (Matthew 22:40) This means if we consistently do these things well—love God fully and love our neighbors as we love ourselves—we will have lived life as He intended.

Branch Living has been designed to help you put God first, and your relationships next. It has been designed to help you love yourself, bringing out the very best that God has seeded in your life.

The plan is the guide; the pathway. It simply sets the course—you run the race. But know, as you run it, you have an entire cheering section rooting you along, wishing you only the very best.

Your fellow Branch Living followers, myself included, are supporting you with prayer. Those who have come before us and now reside in our ultimate heavenly home are also cheering you on.

"Therefore, since we are surrounded by such a great cloud of witnesses, let us throw off everything that hinders and the sin that so easily entangles. And, let us run with perseverance the race marked out for us."
Hebrews 12:1

We are all rooting for you! Go run this race. And, as you go, know that your life is singing your love song right back to God. And He is singing His over you as you go.

Endnotes

1. All Scripture verses from the *New International Version*, 2011.

2. Donald S. Whitney. *Spiritual Disciplines for Christian Life (NavPress, 1997), pg. 19.*

3. Talkaboutgiving.org

4. John Ortberg. *All the Places to Go… How Will You Know? God Has Placed Before You and Open Door. What Will You Do?* (Tyndale House Publishers, 1990.)

5. *Volunteering in the United States*, 2015 U.S. Bureau of Labor Statistics.

6. National Sleep Study Press Release, 2014.

7. Paul Stewart's blog "Thoughts on Faith, Culture, and Missional Living.

8. Greg Laurie's blog "The Power of the Gospel," November 7, 2012.

9. Pope Francis. Daily Mass, April 4, 2015, Vatican Radio.

10. Dr. Charles Stanley, In Touch Ministries, as included in the daily devotional blog "Thoughts about God," posted on June 28, 2015.

Acknowledgments

There are so many people I would like to thank, so many who have enriched my life beyond measure.

But, first, I want to thank God for the unbelievably generous gift of His son Jesus, who makes all things new and all things possible.

I want to thank Jesus for not giving up on me even when I have given up on myself.

I would like to thank my parents, George and Pat Wagner, for raising me in the faith and showing me what a wonderful God we serve.

I especially want to thank my husband, Hal, for helping me grow in the faith each day through his patience, wisdom, and love. How in the world did I ever get so lucky as to have you as my husband and faith partner?

To my kids and their spouses, thank you for knowing me as completely imperfect and loving me in spite of my imperfections. I love you more than words can capture.

To my grandchildren—you unlocked a part of my heart that I did not know existed. How blessed I am by you daily!

And, to Dr. Tim Keller—what a gift you are to this generation. I sit at your feet and try to aborb a portion of your wisdom and insight. You truly ground me and keep me digging deeper and deeper into the faith. I am blessed by you more than I can say.

Appendix

THE PLAN

Month

WHAT?	Jan	Feb	Mar	Apr	May	June	July	Aug	Sept	Oct	Nov	Dec	ANNUAL GOALS
Bond													
Bible reading							X			/	X		360
Devotional				X *Complete*									3 books
Relationships													
Sleepe w/ Kids	3 ->												36
Visit Parents	1 ->												12
Alms													
Volunteer at Shelter													
Tithe													
New													
Complete manuscript	30 ->												360 pages (estimate)
Take class — Careers							X						
Volunteer on community project			X		X			X			X		
Church													
Join Women's Group		X											
Attend 1x per week	4 ->												52
Habits													
Exercise 5x per week	20 ->												260

BRANCH LIVING GOALS
I HOPE TO ACHIEVE THIS YEAR

Bond
   -Read 30 pages of Bible each month
   -Read 2 pages of Devotional each day

Relationships
   -Skype with Kids 3x per month
   -Visit Parents 1x per month
   -Visit one family 1x each 2 months
   -Date night 2ax per month
   -Out with friends 1x per month

Alms
   -Volunteer 1x per month at Shelter
   -$25 per month *extra*
   -Tithe - Church & non-profits

Church
   -Join Women's Group/Bible study
   -Attend 1x per week
   -Join one committee this year

Habits
   -Exercise 5x per week
   -Weight to 130pounds this year

PLOT OUT YOUR GOALS

GOAL	YEAR	ACHIEVE MONTH	WEEK
Bond			
Bible Reading (pages)	360	30	5-10
Devotional	3 books	60	15
Relationships			
Skype with Kids	36x	3x	1x
Visit parents	12x	1x	
Visit one family			
Date night			
Out with friends			
Alms			
Volunteer at Shelter	12x	1x	
$25 per month *extra*			
Tithe			
New			
Complete manuscript (pages)	Approx. 300	25	6
Take Class on Camera	1x		
Volunteer Community Project 1x season	4x	1x per quarter	
Church			
- Join Women's Group/Bible study			
- Attend 1x per week			
- Join one commitee this year			
Habits			
- Exercise 5x per week			
- Weight to 130 pounds this year			

KEEPING TRACK

WEEK OF _March 5th_

	S	M	T	W	T	F	S

Exercise
Bible Reading
Devotion
Write Manuscript -6 pages
Weight to 135

Weekly Tasks

- Volunteer Shelter
- Church Attendance
- Date Night ☺

www.ingramcontent.com/pod-product-compliance
Lightning Source LLC
Chambersburg PA
CBHW051829090426
42736CB00011B/1722